# Reformation & Culture

*Select Lectures*

# Reformation & Culture

*Select Lectures*

STEVEN R. MARTINS

Cántaro Institute

JORDAN STATION, ONTARIO

"I'm pleased to commend *Reformation & Culture: Select Lectures* to the thoughtful Western and Hispanic reader. This is a work in Biblical worldview—the Bible's view of reality, knowledge, and ethics, as Dr. Bahnsen would put it. Learning to think in terms of the Bible's worldview is absolutely critical for Christians if we want to see our cultures transformed and reformed by the gospel and the kingdom-rule of Christ. Steven ably lays out deficiencies in our current cultural landscape—and how the Church has tragically aided in the development of those deficiencies over the past century through dualistic and Pietistic theologies and mindsets—as well as how the Bible's worldview provides much needed answers to those deficiencies. This is a book that deserves careful consideration."

—DAVID A. FORSYTHE, Author of *Vengeance Has Come: A Puritan-Minded Exposition of the Apocalypse for the Modern Church*, An elder at Christ Covenant Church in Selkirk, Manitoba

"I am happy to commend this superb collection of lectures by my dear friend Steven R. Martins. They continue the very best in the reformational tradition which sees the word of God as authoritative not only in our individual lives and in our churches, but out in the wider culture and, in fact, the entire world. The Protestant Reformation was only a beginning. We cannot rest on the laurels of that reformation when we today need another great reformation of biblical authority expressed and implemented everywhere. May this excellent book, *Reformation & Culture: Select Lectures*, contribute to that new reformation."

—P. ANDREW SANDLIN, PhD, Founder & President, Center for Cultural Leadership

"In this collection of lectures, Steven R. Martins provides a wide gamut of information for the Christian reader, touching on church history, doctrine, philosophy, education, and apologetics. For instance, the Spanish Reformation is largely obscure in both English and Spanish-speaking contexts. In response to this, Martins explores the major figures and events of Spain's thwarted Reformation and explains the subsequent negative consequences of the failure of biblical thinking to take hold in the Hispanosphere. In addition, Martins provides a reformational philosophical framework for developing genuinely biblical thinking so that Christians can learn to apply the Bible to every area of life. This book, *Reformation and Culture: Select Lectures*, is especially relevant for the modern church, enabling us to better understand our times and to discern what we ought to do in our Western context."

—MICHAEL WAGNER, PhD, Author of *The Anglosphere's Broken Covenant: Rediscovering the Validity and Importance of the Solemn League and Covenant*

*Dedicated to Esteban Angulo,*
*a dear friend and fellow labourer in the gospel*

cantaroinstitute.org

*Reformation & Culture: Select Lectures*
by Steven R. Martins
Published by Cántaro Publications, a publishing imprint of the
Cántaro Institute, Jordan Station, Ontario, Canada

For volume pricing, please contact
info@cantaroinstitute.org

Library & Archives Canada
ISBN: 978-1-990771-74-3

Printed in the United States of America

# Table of Contents

# Expanded Table of Contents

# Introduction

THE FOLLOWING IS A COLLECTION of select lectures by Rev. Steven R. Martins, founder of the Cántaro Institute, focusing on the themes of reformation and culture. Delivered in various settings and on different occasions, these lectures encompass a wide range of topics. Some address aspects of the history of the Protestant Reformation, offering valuable historical insights and context. Others explore the pressing need for ongoing reformation within the contemporary church, highlighting areas for growth and renewal. Additionally, Martins delves into the relevance of the reformed Christian faith in public culture, examining how we can perceive and pursue cultural renewal in today's society.

This volume, part of the *Cántaro Institute Archives*, is the first in a planned series. Each volume will delve into similar and complementary facets of this theme of reformation and culture, contributing to a deeper understanding and dialogue for the good of God's church. Through these publications, the Cántaro Institute aims to provide a rich resource for scholars, practitioners, and anyone interested in the intersection of the reformed faith, history, and cultural transformation.

It is our hope that as an Institute we can continue to inspire the Christian church by advancing the

Christian worldview for the reformation and renewal of the church and culture. With believers all over the world, we hold firm in our faith to the anticipative fulfillment of Psalm 72:8, "May [Christ] have dominion from sea to sea, and from the River to the ends of the earth!" A prophetic, Scriptural passage that happens to be inscribed on the Peace Tower in Ottawa, Canada, and embraced as Canada's national motto as engraved on our national coat of arms. We confess, faithful to the clear teaching of Scripture, that Christ, today, has dominion (Matt. 28:18), even though His dominion is not yet plainly evident to all. And we await the day when every knee will bow and tongue confess that Jesus Christ is Lord (Phil. 2:10). All that we do, therefore, is to the glory of God and in worship of the everlasting King.

*Soli Deo Gloria*

Cántaro Institute
September 2024
Niagara, Ontario, Canada

# A CALL TO REFORMATION

**Date:** April 24, 2021

**Context:** La Conferencia del Oso

**Setting:** Livestreamed via Youtube and aired live on select Central and South American television channels

## Introductory Remarks

IT IS BOTH MY HONOUR and privilege to open the Cántaro Institute's inaugural conference for Latin America, an event which we hope to organize again in the future. In line with both the mission and vision of the Institute, I thought a most fitting subject for the occasion would be "The Call to Reformation." That is precisely the theme of the inaugural volume of our Iberoamerican Journal for Christian Worldview: *La Fuente*. Let me, however, first introduce the Cántaro Institute before I elaborate on our mission and vision.

The Cántaro Institute is a reformed, evangelical organization committed to the advancement of the Christian worldview for the reformation and renewal of the church and culture. Since our founding, we have had two primary ministry operations: (i) the Anglosphere, and (ii) the Hispanosphere. The Institute was founded to meet a particular need, to respond to a particular challenge that the church at large has struggled to understand; and given where our headquarters are based, that being in Southwestern Ontario, Canada, that challenge looks different within the Anglosphere than it looks within the Hispanosphere. How best to explain this? Perhaps, first, with a look back at our protestant heritage.

## Our Protestant Heritage

The protestant reformation of the 16th century may have started with Martin Luther and the nailing of the 95 Theses on the church door in Wittenberg, but the movement which took the Western world by storm was in all actuality brought about by the recovery of the goodness, beauty, and liberty of the gospel. This was brought to the forefront of everyone's attention as God's people diligently sought to reform themselves according to God's revelatory Word. This "gospel", this good news (Gr. *evangel*) that had been recovered, concerns God's restorative work in creation through His Son Jesus, the Christ, beginning with the human heart, and then overflowing into every cultural and creational aspect. This *comprehensive* gospel—and it really is comprehensive when we consider the scope and extent of Jesus' Lordship—has had a profound influence on the development of Western society, beginning with the efforts of the protestant reformers who diligently worked to apply God's Word to everyday life.[1] However, this recovered gospel, this *biblical* gospel, has been increasingly truncated in the past century from a comprehensive worldview to nothing more than a privatized spirituality, relegating God's redemptive power to the private life of the individual and nothing more. We might describe this as a form of *spiritual decadence*, which has not only been experienced by the West at large, but also most alarmingly, by the Western church.

The spiritual condition of Ibero-America, or the Hispanosphere, has not been any better—if we could even consider it spiritually *decadent*. For something to decay, we have to presuppose that there was something previously good and healthy that was subject to decay. And that cannot quite be said of Ibero-America. The reason for this is that the region had never experienced the fully-bloomed protestant reformation of the 16th century. The embers of the reformation had been censored, martyred, and exiled from Spanish territories with such ferocity that Roman Catholicism was all

---

1. See Vishal Mangalwadi, *The Book That Made Your World: How the Bible Created the Soul of Western Civilization* (Nashville, TN.: Thomas Nelson, 2012).

that there was. Romanism was essentially championed with much bravado by both the Pope and the Spanish monarchy, declaring it the only *permissible* religion for man. The inevitable result of such religious tyranny was the propagation of Rome's *false* gospel, principally that of *works-plus-grace*, and that meant that the Iberoamerican culture could never experience the fruits of a distinctly biblical worldview brought about by the exposition and application of the gospel. Given the scholastic dualism of Roman Catholicism, which regards some things as sacred (the sphere of grace) and others as neutral (the sphere of nature)—think of the writings of Scripture as "sacred" and the pagan apostate philosophies of the Greeks as "neutral"—and that grace somehow perfects nature, though they can never *truly* be reconciled,[2] the majority of the Iberoamerican people to this day have fallen prey to religious syncretism, including much of the protestant church.[3] On a visit to Cuba a few years ago, I witnessed, for example, several religious syntheses, Santeria being one most common. There is a significant plurality of Christianized syntheses all across Iberoamerica. It almost forces one to ask,

---

2.    Willem J. Ouweneel, *The World is Christ's: A Critique of Two Kingdoms Theology* (Jordan Station, ON.: Paideia Press, 2017), 44; John M. Frame, *A History of Western Philosophy and Theology* (Phillipsburg, NJ.: P&R Publishing, 2015), 145.

3.    Miguel Núñez, *El Poder de la Palabra para Transformar una Nación* (Medellín, Colombia: Poiema Publicaciones, 2016), 10.

What has happened here? What has happened to the truth?

For both the Western and Iberoamerican church, given what has been witnessed most prominently in the past century, the mission to advance the kingdom of God has been hampered due to a *misunderstanding* of the gospel. On the one hand, the gospel has been limited in its scope and nature; and on the other, the gospel has been polluted by religious syncretism. As long as this misunderstanding of the gospel prevails, neither the Western, nor the Iberoamerican people and their culture will experience the renewal and transformation that the true gospel brings. What then lies before us? To put it bluntly: *a sure disaster*—that is, if things were to remain as they are. As God's people, called to be the light and salt of the earth (Matt. 5:13-16) we are not progressing as we should in terms of (i) advancing the gospel in the hearts of men, and (ii) preserving God's creational law-order in their minds.[4]

It ought to be of no surprise then that we are where we are. After all, there has been a serious disconnect

---

4. "In [the church] there is a preserving force to keep the rest of society from utter corruption. If [the church] were not scattered among men, the race would putrefy... We are to remove the darkness of ignorance, sin, and sorrow. Christ has lighted us that we may enlighten the world... God intends his grace to be as conspicuous as a city built on the mountain's brow", Charles H. Spurgeon, *The Gospel of the Kingdom: A Popular Exposition of the Gospel according to Matthew* (New York, NY.: The Baker & Taylor Co., 1893), 45-46.

between the heart and the mind, and by that I mean that, while there has certainly been a genuine heart commitment to Jesus and His Lordship amongst God's people, there remains today a great deal of ignorance as it concerns *how our thinking* should be subject to His Lordship. And whether or not we would like to believe it, it is for that reason that our public witness has become compromised at best (and that is putting it generously), because despite the stated intention of the church to live according to God's truth, it has partitioned off much of our public life from our witness. A few months ago, for example, while leading a Bible study, I taught on the passage of 1 Peter 2:18-19. Within the context of that passage I spoke on the glorification of Christ through our work. Apparently, the "idea" that you could "bring God to work with you", as one of our students had put it, was so *novel* that it began to revolutionize the way he saw his work. It brought about a greater understanding of his respective vocation.

## The Solution We Seek

But simply "bringing God to work with you" is not the solution that we have been seeking, it is not the vision that we have so long sought after, that is, in terms of *how* exactly God's people ought to *live* in this fallen world. It goes much deeper than that: *It is to rethink this world entirely.* For example, the fallen world system has led much of the church to believe in the sacred-secular divide, it is a framework that is akin to its pre-

Reading of Voltaire's tragedy, *Orphan of China*, in the salon
of Marie Thérèse Rodet Geoffrin in 1755, by Lemonnier, c. 1812

decessor of the nature-grace framework found in the
medieval scholasticism of Rome. I will avoid getting
into the details for the sake of time, but it suffices to
say that this sacred-secular dualism finds its roots in
the Enlightenment of the 17th and 18th centuries.[5] That
philosophical movement had as its three central tenets
the (1) use of reason; (2) the scientific method; and
(3) progress, which the three joined together would
supposedly help with the creation of better societies
and better people. What it has instead done is *mortify* the soul of the West (Ibero-America included) by
removing the people further away from the God who

---

5.  See Herman Dooyeweerd, *Roots of Western Culture: Pagan,
    Secular, and Christian Options* (Jordan Station, ON.: Paideia
    Press, 2012).

created them and who calls them to repentance and covenant faithfulness. We might call all these apostate philosophical systems "tools of mortification", and this is not to be confused with Romans 8:13, which reads "For if you live according to the flesh you will die, but if by the Spirit you put to death the deeds of the body, you will live" (ESV). Whereas God's Word instructs us towards the *mortification of the flesh*, which is to put to death the deeds of our *sinful nature*, the world and its apostate philosophies indoctrinates man in the *mortification of the spirit*, putting to death any thought and deed that makes reference to the true God, our Creator. And by replacing God with created man, society has paved its own way to ruin, the inevitable result of its "zombification", that is to say, spiritually dead men with living, animate bodies.

Returning to my point, if our world system has thus established the sacred-secular divide with such widespread success that it seems only natural to every person, even amongst God's people, then we need to break from this world's mould in order to view and interpret this world rightly according to God's written revelation. As opposed to adopting the sacred-secular divide devised from the fallen and depraved minds of men, the Bible teaches us with such clarity and without apology that all things in this created world are sacred, and that every creational interaction between man and creation ought to be sacred. Now, we can admittedly say that this is not the world we see before us. Secularized human institutions do not appear *sacred*. Medical institutions with their abortion and euthanasia services do not appear *sacred*. Political institutions with their false promises and gross abuses do not appear *sacred*. The reason for all this is that man has made what ought to be sacred, *profane*.[6] Our sinfulness, our fallen condition, our depravity, has led us to make a monumental mess of this beautiful world and what God intended for it. There is no fault to be found in the spheres themselves, whether the state, family, charity, market, academy, or society.[7] *Man is the problem*, his *heart* is the problem, for where sin reigns, there we find only death, ruin, and destruction. It is only by the mercy of God that we have not succumbed entirely to our own self-destruction.

And yet, in spite of the corruption that marks our world, nothing can possibly be done to remove it from Christ's domain. Man might renounce God with all his fervour and strength, but renouncing the air we breathe does not make the air non-existent, nor does it free us from the necessity to breathe air. Yes, it is true, man *cannot* blot out God and His truth, just as much as he cannot blot out his *need* for Him. He is a creature

---

6.  R.J. Rushdoony, "Salvation and Godly Rule: Prophet, Priest & King." *Pocket College*. Accessed March 6, 2017. http://www.pocketcollege.com/transcripts/091%20-%20 Salvation%20and%20Godly%20Rule/RR136AG62.html.

7.  See Abraham Kuyper, *Sphere Sovereignty*, trans. George Kamps (The Free University, 1880).

of God, created in the image of God, breathing the air of God, as he lives in the cosmos created by God. This is how we can understand that profound and powerful passage written by the apostle Paul, "For by [Christ] all things were created, in heaven and on earth, visible and invisible, whether thrones or dominions or rulers or authorities—all things were created through him and for him" (Col. 1:16).

For those of you who have studied computer sciences or videogame engineering, you might be able to understand the ridiculousness of the sinful man's predicament. It is like a character in a game that refuses to believe that the game has a creator, and that the game follows certain rules, and within this context the character goes on to try to change those rules to create his own kind of game, a different virtual reality. The idea is ridiculous, of course, because a video game requires a designer. That code had to come from somewhere, much like a computer system requires a programmer. And whatever was built with that code technically belongs to someone and is meant to fulfill the purpose it was given. Of course, our reality is not a video game, we are not living in the Matrix, like that 1999 movie with Keanu Reeves. Reality is far grander than that. But the principle remains the same: *Our created reality has a Creator.* To deny this fact is to forfeit our intelligence, and to adopt the foolishness brought about by our own sinfulness. Abraham Kuyper put it well when he said: "No single piece of our mental world is to be hermetically sealed off from the rest, and there is not a square inch in the whole domain of our human existence over which Christ, who is Sovereign over all, does not cry: Mine!"[8]

What must be done then? If we have before us such a ridiculous mess of a world, and we have ourselves such a mangled conception as to (i) what the gospel is, and (ii) how we ought to live in this world, to *where* and to *what* must we turn to? I like what the late Christian thinker H. Evan Runner wrote (1916-2002) in the fourth volume of his collected works. His answer articulates precisely that which the protestant reformers turned to: "The solution is to allow the Scriptures themselves to speak to us again. The Word of God pierces to the very heart with its truth."[9]

## The Reforming Spirit

Think back to the sixteenth century, a period of time when God's truth had been obscured by the religious humanistic teachings of the Roman Catholic Church. It was not that God's truth had been obscured to the extent that it had been hidden completely, for it had been made clearly evident to all by means of God's cre-

---

8.   Abraham Kuyper, inaugural lecture at the Free University of Amsterdam, October 20, 1880, quoted in *Abraham Kuyper: A Centennial Reader*, ed. James D. Bratt (Grand Rapids: Eerdmans, 1998), 488.

9.   H. Evan Runner, *The Collected Works of H. Evan Runner, Vol. 4: The Urgent Need for Christian Renewal* (Jordan Station, ON.: Paideia Press, 2021), 51.

ation and His Word, thus leaving man with no excuse. It is rather that Romanism made every effort to blind the people to what is plain and evident to all. At the root of it, what had occurred was that the base motive of pagan thought had successfully corrupted the Roman Catholic institution, and this was thanks to its implementation and synthesis. You see, the very moment that Greek philosophy was erroneously equated with divine truth (which can be traced back as far as to the patristics), a door was opened for the underlying motive of all godless, apostate thought to infiltrate the church. This is the godless motive that we find in the third chapter of Genesis, of created man seeking to be *radically autonomous*, that is to say, independent from God and His law, and to be like God in a manner that was inappropriate for a creature. Medieval scholasticism, and Thomas Aquinas in particular, cemented that synthesis in the thought and life of the Roman Catholic Church, and that synthesis of (i) God's revealed truth, and (ii) the fallen thought of man, led the way to the rendering of a monstrosity, the inevitable result of attempting to synthesize the THESIS with the ANTITHESIS. No doubt Satan was pleased with the supposed "dimming" of the light of truth, but as with all his efforts, his attempt to manipulate man to his own will is nothing but futility, and for those caught unawares, his will since his fall has been to utterly destroy God's handiwork.

Martin Luther hammering his *95 Theses* in 1517,
by Ferdinand Willem Pauwels, 1872

But thanks be to God that by His mercy and grace, and according to His divine providence, He led pious men, *learned* men, to the truth of His Word. And so necessary is this Word of God for men, that if we were not to have this Word, mankind would be left without a true interpretation of God's creation. It is, after all, because of sin's corrupting influence upon the minds of men that a written revelation was deemed necessary for man. And what a joy this was for the reformers, who discovered the truth, not outside of, but within God's Word alone. In the Word they discovered the truth *unadulterated*; truth which exposed the lies of the papacy, the humanistic direction of its traditions, and the religious prostitution of Romanism. If only the fire of the reformation had continued to burn in Spain, that country so determined to be the champion of Roman Catholicism; a country which had such a profound influence on its colonies in the New World. It was not enough for the Inquisition to seek the destruction of the protestant church in Europe, its operations extended as far as Latin America.

Now, while I can certainly bemoan the fact that the reformation within Spanish borders had been quelled—and I do feel about that much anguish as a fellow Iberoamerican—I believe can accomplish far more good today by instead speaking of those valiant men who gave their lives to such an important cause.[10] It was not merely a matter of standing for religious liberty, but rather the vanquishing of the darkness with the clear light of God's Word. And while there are many factors to consider, and many people to call to our attention, the little they accomplished was for the most part made possible by a man named *Julianillo*, whom we could describe as a light and humble breeze that gave fuel to the growing fire of the reformation. Now, when I say what "little they accomplished", it is certainly meant from man's finite perspective, because in the sight of God, their small achievements were great and monumental.[11] In retrospect, it is precisely because

---

10. *Editor's Note: The following are short summaries in comparison to the later depth and elaboration provided in the fourth chapter, "The Reformation & the Spanish". Excuse thus any apparent and minor repetitions and appreciate the added depth that follows in the fourth chapter.*

11. See Thomas M'Crie, *History of the Spanish Reformation: Progress & Suppression in the 16ᵗʰ Century* (Jordan Station, ON., Cántaro Publications, 2023).

there *was* a Spanish reformation, as short-lived as it may have been, that we have today the Bible in the Spanish vernacular tongue, particularly, the Reina-Valera Bible translation. On that matter I do intend to return. But I must first make mention of Julianillo, and some of the others involved in the Spanish reformation, in order to bring to light the reformational spirit that not only unified them, but produced within them a willingness to be martyrs for Christ.

And what martyrs we need for our day, not in the literal sense, for we live in an altogether different time, and the challenges and threats we face as God's church are wholly different, but we need men and women who are willing to be cut off from society, to be cast out socially and persecuted for advocating and defending God's truth in an increasingly depraved world. I do not mean a willful, self-imposed exile, for that accomplishes nothing. Our churches are already guilty as charged when it comes to "cultural retreatism". I mean boldly proclaiming and defending God's truth in every area of life, to such an extent that the world has no choice but to respond to our prophetic witness. And we know that that response can only either be repentance or hostility. The witness of the first disciples in the book of Acts shows us what awaits the faithful. Are we to think that we are special? That we are the exception? No. We too may suffer persecution. In fact, persecution, in whatever form it may take, is to be expected (Matt. 10:16-25).

Like what we see in Scripture, God can use any

man to stir the church up to its feet (think of Stephen), just like He used Julianillo to fan the flames of the reformational spirit across Spain—a spirit that spurs us on to live before God in every respect (the Latin, *Coram Deo*). Julián Hernández was his proper name, born in Valladolid, Spain in the sixteenth century. Because he was not a member of the high class, or occupied a distinguished position in the world of men, not much data is found concerning his life. But this much we do know: While Julianillo was born in Spain, he was raised in Germany, the country that produced the protestant reformer, Martin Luther. At one point in his life, Julianillo learned to work in the printing industry as a typesetter, and given his position this allowed him to travel to various parts of Europe where he would eventually learn, study, and adopt the teachings of the protestant reformers. Later in life, it is believed that between the years 1550 and 1559, Julianillo had managed to smuggle into Spain more than two barrels-full of Spanish New Testament translations by Juan Pérez de Pineda. This was often at great risk to his own life, for this act alone was punishable by death by the Spanish Inquisition.

As one reflects on Julianillo's contribution, which has been regarded by some to be unimportant according to the "lofty" standards of the world of men, his contribution to the life of the church proved to be crucial, for without his contribution there would have

Persecution of Protestants by the Spanish Inquisition
in the 16th Century, various artists

been very little momentum in the protestant centers of
Seville and Valladolid. And his contribution was not
just in the act of smuggling New Testament translations into Spain, it was the giving up of his life as well.
As we might have expected, Julianillo was eventually
found out by the Spanish Inquisition, and as a result,
he was burned alive at the stake for all in Seville to see.
But worthy of mentioning, and this is not unimportant, he did not leave this earth quietly like a mouse. He
left more like a defiant lion. His final moments were
not as some weak and frail thing, though his bones had
been dislocated, and his body had suffered great tor-
ture. Strengthened by the Spirit of God, as he was carried to the stake, he sang out loud for all to hear: "The
friars go vanquished, they go vanquished! The wolves
go running, running they go..." (*¡Vencidos van los frail-*

*es, vencidos van! Corridos van los lobos, corridos van...*).[12]

As I think about martyrs, another reformer comes to mind: Constantino Ponce de la Fuente (1502-1560). Unlike Julianillo, Constantino was a notable figure given his prestigious position within the Roman Catholic Church. Born in the province of Cuenca, and having received a theological education at the Universidad de Alcalá, he served as the principal orator in Seville's cathedral. He was largely popular with the people, and was honoured for his many writings. While Constantino did what he could to uphold a Catholic image of himself, he had adopted the convictions of the protestant faith, and having become a protestant in secret, made it his mission to instruct the people in biblical truth through his own sermons and writings. He did this without mentioning Luther, the protestants, or any particular name, reference, or label that could possibly incriminate him. Amidst his various writings, his most popular were the *Confesión de un Pecador* and *Suma de Doctrina Cristiana*. And we would discover later that his teachings and writings went far beyond Seville and towards the Mesoamerican missionfield, where, for example, the Nahua and Zacatecas of Mexico were being

---

12. See Marcelino Menéndez y Pelayo, *Historia de los Heterodoxos Españoles*; John E. Longhurst, *Julian Hernandez: Protestant Martyr*, Bibliothèque d'Humanisme et Renaissance: Librairie Droz, 90-118.; Martin de Roa, *Historia de la Compañía de Jesús en Andalucía*.

taught the basics of the Christian faith.[13] What Constantino had attempted was to reform the church from within, believing that nothing other than the Word of God could reform the church, because only the Word of God can change hearts and lives. Unfortunately, like Julianillo and many other protestants, Constantino was found out. The Inquisition had acquired secret writings of his that were explicitly Lutheran, or protestant, and that was enough for his condemnation given that he refused to recant. Perhaps as a mercy afforded to him by God, he was spared a public execution as he died of illness in his cell.[14] Whatever the people thought of him at the time, and irregardless of his lowly death, it cannot be denied that he was a great spiritual giant in the land of the reformers, a true martyr in the church of Christ.

I must now briefly mention Casiodoro de Reina (1520-1594), and his disciple Cipriano de Valera (1531-1602). Reina, like Valera, were monks at San Isidoro in Seville, and both had arrived at protestant convictions. It is believed that Reina was the one responsible for organizing some of the protestant gath-

---

13. Andrew L. Wilson, "The Unfortunate Fate of Luther in the Ibero-American World" in *Studies in Luther* (USA: Lutheran Forum, Summer 2009), 32.

14. Marcelino Menéndez Pelayo, *Historia de los Heterodoxos Españoles.*; A. Gordon Kinder, *Casiodoro de Reina: Spanish Reformer of the Sixteenth Century* (London, UK., Tamesis Books Limited, 1975), 9.

Bildnis Cassiodoro de Reina (Reyna) (lat. Cassiodorus Reinius),
by Peter Fehr (1681-1740)

erings in Seville, though the daily pastoral duties were
passed on to another, a particular physician that would
later be caught by the Inquisition.[15] Before they were
found out, however, Reina and Valera managed to
flee Spain. As a result, both spent some time in John
Calvin's Geneva, but eventually both made their way
to England, where refuge had been offered to persecuted protestants. While there Reina planted a church
in London with the endorsement of the queen of En-

15. Steven R. Martins, "Christobal Losada" in Deborah
Alcock, *The Spanish Brothers* (Jordan Station, ON.: Cántaro
Publications, 2020), 78.

gland, and that church would continue under Valera's leadership when the Inquisition manufactured a scandal that forced Reina to flee.[16] Throughout this time, from the moment of his departure from Spain to his travels in Europe, Reina managed to complete the first Spanish translation of the entire Bible in 1569, which would be titled the *Biblia del Oso*, precisely from where our inaugural conference draws its name from.[17] Valera, shortly after, published a revised and edited version of Reina's translation, the *Biblia del Cántaro* in 1602.

## A Significant Undertaking

I have only mentioned four reformers, and there are several more to consider, but you will notice something that they all shared in common: The Word of God was their life's *fount*. The Word of God was their *foundation*. And the Word of God was their *passion*. Why? Because of what it is (the inspired Word of God), and who it reveals (the Triune God). The reformation would not have been possible if not for God's Word and its translation into the vernacular. I mention all this to make a simple point: The spirit of the reformers was to singularly restore the Word of God to its rightful place, that being, as man's *ultimate* authority. It is, after all, from the Scriptures that we learn of the *true gospel*. It is from the Scriptures that we learn of *man's place in the world under God*. And it is from the Scriptures

16. Gordon A. Kindle, *Casiodoro de Reina*, 27-34.

17. *La Conferencia del Oso*.

that we learn *how we ought to live*. Unless the church understands the centrality of God's Word as it relates to its mission, as it relates to its calling to be the light and salt of the earth, and within the context of the *whole* of life, much of what the church accomplishes will be nothing more than a light hidden under a basket, and like salt that has lost its taste. We need to break free from the error of relegating our faith to a *privatized* spirituality. We need to rediscover what it means to live under the Lordship of Christ, who reigns over *every inch of creation*. There are no independent kings in this world, *nothing* is fenced off from the authority of Christ (Matt. 28:18; 1 Cor. 15:27-28). *Everything* is subject to Him. I think back to the words of Runner, who wrote:

> Since the creation structure is integral, that is, has a root-unity that is religion, or our covenant-walk before God, the direction of life, be it the rebellion of sin or a newly learned obedience to the Word of God in the Spirit, will be radical, that is, will be evidenced in *every* aspect of life.[18]

In other words, because we live in God's world, because there is a *structure* to every aspect of creation, our creational interaction will be religious in its *direction*, either in worship to God or expressed as rebellion against Him. *Everything* we do is religious. The question we must ask then is not *What* are we doing? For

---

18. Runner, *The Collected Works of H. Evan Runner, Vol. 4*, 91.

The beginning of the Gospel of John from a copy of the 1526 edition
of William Tyndale's New Testament at the British Library.

both a Christian and an unbeliever can do much of the
same line of work *structurally-speaking*. The question is
*How?* How are we doing all that we do in the respective
spheres? And I mean that *directionally-speaking*. Are we
doing all things *Christianly*, or according to the same
spirit as this fallen world? The point of the matter is:
We need to break free from the mould of this world
system, and we need to live in light of the Scriptures,
in a *total* comprehensive sense. *That* is the vision, *that*
is the objective, *that* is where we would like to be as
God's people, because by the time that we arrive there,

by the time we understand this, we will not be doing anything else but be intimately involved with cultivating creation into a godly civilization—where God's Word is adhered to as our ultimate authority. But to get there? We need a *reformation*. We need to take up that same reformational spirit, fan it to flame, and carry that torch far and wide, from our homes, to our churches, to our legislatures, and beyond.

Practically speaking then, what must we do? That is the right question to ask. There is a simple answer I can give for now: *We must restore the Word of God to its rightful place, as our ultimate authority.* But, of course, it sounds much simpler than it really is. When we give this some thought, we realize that there is, in fact, much that we need to unlearn. All the baggage from this world's fallen thinking that has become entrenched within us needs to be worked out of our system, and we need to replace that with *biblical* thinking, that is to say, a way of thinking that is wisely informed and directed by the Word of God. If you are thinking to yourself that this is too far great a task to accomplish overnight, you are right. We are talking about a comprehensive reformation, and such a reformation requires time, it requires effort, it requires *everything* from ourselves as persons and as a church community. It may even take generations! Let me, therefore, give a few thoughts of what we must do if we hope to see such a reformation, one much more profound and robust than what we are already seeing in the world today.

Firstly, the principles of the reformation need to be embraced by church leadership, because until the time comes that the true biblical gospel is preached from the pulpits, and I do not mean a *truncated* version of the gospel, but the gospel as it relates to *every creational aspect*, we should not expect there to be any meaningful reformation, at least as it concerns the full realization of the church's mission. If we feel inadequate for this task as church leaders, this should not be reason to abandon hope, but rather it should serve as motivation to press forward in our training and development. If this was not, in truth, a lofty task, a significant undertaking, then it would not be as glorious. But the conditions are absolutely ripe for God to be most glorified. In view of this, we then need to be exhorted. If we, as church leaders, make no effort to take the lead in this, then the people will not follow, because at the end of the day, whether we like it or not, the people will emulate whatever their leaders *model* to them.

Secondly, the church needs to look at recovering its educational mandate. As it concerns discipleship, we have the mistaken notion that our task is to simply educate our members in the core doctrines of our faith, but this is only the first step of many. We are not just preparing good spiritual Christians, we are to prepare good Christian *businessmen*, good Christian *politicians*, good Christian *architects*, good Christian *policemen*, good Christian *philosophers*, etc. We need to stop limiting ourselves to solely the theological discipline and take seriously what it means to have a worldview, and the absolute necessity of a *biblical* worldview.

Thirdly, as it will take time for the church to recover its educational mandate, and to launch initiatives toward fulfilling that mandate, we need other Christian organizations, confessional organizations, to rise up and partner with each other to work toward assisting the church in its reformation and mission. Even if the Cántaro Institute were to become as large as many of the leading organizations today, whether that be Ligonier, Founders Ministries, Answers in Genesis, etc., we would still be a small fish before the vast need facing the church today. We need to work together, hence why we have various ministries participating in our conference today; and we need to always be in the process of reformation, as the reformational phrase goes, *ecclesia semper reformanda.*

As I bring our first session to a close, I am aware of the fact that I have not provided a quick and immediate solution, because the truth is, there is not one. But I *can* say with certainty that we have at least *started* the conversation, and I hope and pray that the other sessions of this conference will further that conversation and instill in us a response to action, for there is a great call before us, a call to reformation. May God find us faithful in our response to the great need facing the church today.

*Soli Deo Gloria.*

# TAKING STEPS TOWARDS REFORMATION

**Date:** October 27, 2021

**Context:** Semper Reformanda, Escuela Superior de Estudios
Bíblicos y Teológicos

**Setting:** Online Class Lectures

## Introductory Remarks

BROTHERS AND SISTERS of the reformation in El Salvador and Central America, it is my privilege to participate in this conference on "The Reformation and Transformation of Culture", organized by the Christian Institution of Higher Education, Semper Reformanda. Before I proceed with our subject matter, I wanted to express my gratitude to Semper Reformanda's Director, Rev. Javier Dominguez, as well as tonight's facilitator, Oscar Perez, and my dear friend and colleague, Daniel

Salgado Herrarte. While our time is short this evening, my hope is that the seed planted tonight may result in a blessed abundance of fruit that would spread the seeds of the reformation everywhere in Ibero-America, as well as the West. This is, in fact, the purpose of this lecture: to inform you, to inspire you, and to assist you in taking hold of the inheritance of our spiritual forefathers, that is to say, the work of those saints who have come before us, which is the *reforming* of all of life. And to fulfill the latter in particular, what we require, in truth, is the collective effort of the Christian community in Ibero-America and the West, because what we are about to discuss this evening is not merely the matter of *personal* spiritual reformation, but the *collective* reformation of Ibero-America, the West, and their respective cultures. As we are about to see, reformation work is not *easy* labour, that is to say, it is not a *mission* of relative ease—and yes, it *is* in fact "the mission" of the church, because contrary to popular thought today, the reformation of culture is very much a *part* of the Great Commission (Matt. 28:18-20).

It is timely that this lecture is taking place only four days before Reformation Day (October 31). A time when the Christian (reformed) church celebrates their protestant roots, commemorating the nailing of the *95 Theses* of Martin Luther, which sparked a reformation across all of Europe beginning in Wittenberg.[1] While

---

1.    See Michael Reeves, *The Unquenchable Flame: Discovering the Heart of the Reformation* (Nashville, TN.: B&H Academic, 2010).

Portrait of John Calvin in his library from *Ioannis Calvini Noviodunensis Opera omnia: in novem tomos digesta*. Amstelodami: Apud viduam Joannis Jacobi Schipperi, 1671

this reformation had more to do with the re-discovery and restoration of the doctrines of grace, or to put it more simply, the core of the *biblical gospel*, its spirit, articulated in the five *Solas*, have a larger scope than simply that of soteriology (the doctrine of salvation). We can see some of that in Luther and Calvin's attempts to discard the manner of "Christian" thinking of the medieval scholastics (I put the word "Christian" in quotation marks because it is not *distinctly* Christian), and in its place the pursuit of the reformation of Christian thought, but their attempts were, for the most part, undone by their successors.[2] In any case, the five *Solas*,

---

2.  Willem J. Ouweneel, *Wisdom for Thinkers: Introduction to Christian Philosophy* (Jordan Station, ON.: Paideia Press, 2014), 24.

articulated traditionally as

(i) Saved by the Grace of God alone (*Sola Gratia*)
(ii) through Faith alone (*Sola Fide*)
(iii) in Christ alone (*Solus Christus*)
(iv) according to Scripture alone (*Sola Scriptura*)
(v) for the glory of God alone (*Soli Deo Gloria*)"[3]

can be expanded in its scope because of the comprehensive nature of the gospel.[4] And if that seems new to you, it is largely because this comprehensive understanding and application of the gospel has been lost to most of the church today. So for that reason, we are not only going to look at the question, Why does Ibero-America (and the West) need a cultural reformation and transformation? But also, What is the gospel? What is culture? What is the relationship between gospel and culture? And after having explored all these things, we can then look towards some of the steps that the collective church can take towards realizing a *cultural* reformation. Much of what I have to share with you has been the result of tedious study under various Christian leaders and thinkers, some in the realm of apologetics

---

3. See Keith Mathison, "The Five Solas", *Reformation Bible College*. Accessed June 5, 2021, https://reformationbiblecollege.org/blog/the-five-solas.

4. See P. Andrew Sandlin, *The Full Gospel: A Biblical Vocabulary of Salvation* (USA: Chalcedon Inc., 2001).

such as Cornelius Van Til,[5] Greg L. Bahnsen,[6] and John M. Frame,[7] others in the realm of Christian philosophy such as Abraham Kuyper,[8] Herman Dooyeweerd,[9] and H. Evan Runner,[10] and other names worth mentioning are Joseph Boot,[11] Miguel Núñez,[12] and Willem J. Ouweneel,[13] all of whom have publications available in both English and Spanish today (or who will soon, at least, within the next few years). Thus, if after this lecture you would like to learn more, these are some of

5.  See Cornelius Van Til, *Christian Apologetics*, second ed. (Phillipsburg, NJ.: P&R Publishing, 2003).

6.  See Greg L. Bahnsen, *Pushing the Antithesis: The Apologetic Methodology of Greg L. Bahnsen* (USA: American Vision, 2007).

7.  See John M. Frame, *A History of Western Philosophy and Theology* (Phillipsburg, NJ.: P&R Publishing, 2015).

8.  See Abraham Kuyper, *Sphere Sovereignty*, trans. George Kamps (The Free University, 1880).

9.  See Herman Dooyeweerd, *Roots of Western Culture: Pagan, Secular and Christian Options*, trans. John N. Kraay and Bernard Zylstra (Toronto, ON.: Wedge Publishing Foundation, 1979).

10. See H. Evan Runner, *The Collected Works of H. Evan Runner*, Vols. 1-4 (Jordan Station, ON.: Paideia Press, 2021).

11. See Joseph Boot, *The Mission of God: A Manifesto of Hope for Society* (Toronto, ON.: Ezra Press, 2016).

12. See Miguel Núñez, *El Poder de la Palabra para Transformar una Nación: Un llamado bíblico e histórico a la iglesia latinoamericana* (Medellín, Colombia: Poiema Publicaciones, 2016).

13. See Willem J. Ouweneel, *Wisdom for Thinkers*.

the references that form the foundation of what I will be discussing here today.

## The Question

We begin with the first question, Why does Ibero-America (and the West) require a cultural reformation and transformation? And, I would add, why in that order? First, concerning the need for a cultural reformation and transformation: When comparing Latin America with the Anglosphere, there are evident differences in terms of the history of thought in both spheres. In Ibero-America, for example, we witness to a far greater degree various syntheses involving explicitly idolatrous religion, Roman Catholicity, and modern philosophies, than what we witness in the Anglosphere. That is not to say that such things do not exist in the Anglosphere, idolatrous religion is everywhere for that matter, but the place that these syntheses have occupied in the development of nations and cultures in Ibero-America has resulted in a very different rendering than what we see in English-speaking countries. For example, we do not see animism, Mariology, Santería, Liberation Theology, Chavismo, or other specific syntheses unique to the Ibero-American context ingrained in the development of the Western Anglosphere.[14] We certainly see idolatrous religion in the public culture of the West, all the more since it departed from its re-

---

14. Núñez, *El Poder de la Palabra para Transformar una Nación*, 10.

ligious foundations, but in contrast to Ibero-America, when we speak about the foundation of the West, we really mean the Judeao-Christian worldview. This is not at all the case with Ibero-America. And the reason for this differentiation is largely due to the presence and influence of the protestant reformation in the early development stages of the Anglosphere versus the absence of it in Ibero-America. As a result of the Spanish Inquisition's efforts in the sixteenth century, and the counter-reformation that followed, the protestant reformation had little to no influence on the development of Iberoamerican religion (faith) and society, largely because of its absence. On the contrary, because of the influence of the Roman Catholic worldview, which is dualistic given its nature-grace scheme, the absence of the protestant reformation gave way to all sorts of syntheses. Before proceeding further, let me define what I mean by the terms "nature-grace scheme" and "syntheses", terms that find their fuller meaning in the Christian philosophy of Herman Dooyeweerd.

What is the *nature-grace* scheme? According to Dooyeweerd, there are four religious ground-motives that have governed the thinking of philosophers over the course of human history, these can be found in his book *Roots of Western Culture*.[15] Out of the four ground-motives, one is the nature-grace scheme. Before proceeding to answering the question, however, let me define the term "religious ground-motive." It means

---

15. See Dooyeweerd, *Roots of Western Culture*.

*Scuola di Atene, The School of Athens*, fresco, 1511, by Raphael (1483–1520)

the basic (*ground*) motivation (*motive*) that underlies all that we think and do.[16] Dooyeweerd traces this back to the ancient Greek philosophers with the first scheme being matter-form (he actually traces this further back than the philosophers, but we will stick to this first provided ground-motive).[17] For the Greeks, most especially Plato (428–348 BC) and Aristotle (384–322 BC), they believed that above this world there was a higher world, and this was articulated as follows: The world we live in today is the world of *matter*, and this world is modeled after the higher world, the world of *forms*.[18] For example, if you look at a tree, you know that it is a tree. You can also tell if it is a good tree or

16. Ouweneel, *Wisdom for Thinkers*, 27.

17. See Dooyeweerd, *Roots of Western Culture*.

18. Frame, *A History of Western Philosophy and Theology*, 64.

a bad tree. A tree that is withering is not the same as a full-grown tree that is healthy. The philosophers argued that in the world of the forms there is true *tree-ness*. But there is always a disconnect between this world of matter and the world of forms in the sense that this world proved resistant towards being *formed*, and this produced an irreconcilable dualism between the two planes of reality.

Now, the reason I started with the matter-form scheme of the Greeks is because the medieval scholastics of the Roman Catholic Church adopted and integrated the Greek matter-form scheme with their *nature-grace* scheme. This is what we call a "synthesis", defined as "the combination of ideas to form a theory or system." Aquinas and Anselm are textbook examples of being proponents of this nature-grace scheme. How do we understand this nature-grace scheme? For Aquinas and the scholastics, there was the plane of *nature*, which consists of natural reason, the Greek philosophers, their matter-form scheme, the natural world, and the institution of the state; and then there was the plane of *grace*, which consists of God's revelation, faith, Scripture, eternal life, salvation, and the church.[19] Here is a better way of understanding this division—a scheme that we are more familiar with in terms of its name and how it is manifested today—the sacred and the secular. Secularization, however, finds its roots in the third ground-motive, which we shall shortly visit.

---

19. Ibid., 145.

In the scholastic nature-grace scheme, however, Christians could, quite simply, take Greek thought, or any natural thought that has nothing to do with the Scriptures, just as it is (as if it were to be free and undefiled by the influence of sin) and treat it as a supplement to God's revelatory Word.

This scheme governed the thought of much of Iberoamerican history because of the significant influence of the Roman Catholic Church, and it was for this reason that instead of turning to the Scriptures for the building blocks of a distinctly Christian worldview, upon which we could build a godly civilization— whether it was in the realms of the state, the family, the church, the marketplace, etc.—the people turned to the natural philosophers, the politicians, the shamans, and everything else under the sun. It is no surprise then that Iberoamerican culture is what it is today when we consider (i) the *history* of its thought, (ii) *what governed* the thought of the people, and most particularly (iii) *what governed* the thought of the national leaders of several Iberoamerican states. The *Gran Colombia* (1819–30), for example, was formed by the efforts of Simon Bolívar, the celebrated liberator believed to be more significant than Alexander the Great in terms of his military accomplishments.[20] Bolívar, for those unaware, was deeply influenced by Enlightenment thought, that movement of the eighteenth century that

---

20. See Marie Arana, *Bolivar: American Liberator* (New York, NY.: Simon & Schuster, 2014).

A portrait of Simon Bolivar, *El Libertador* (the Liberator)
of South America, from the Miraflores Palace, Caracas, Venezuela

elevated "reason" as the solution to all of man's ills, while discarding God in His totality from the equation.[21] It was the rise of the third religious ground-motive, the *nature-freedom* scheme, which, to summarize, posited *nature* as the higher plane: the deterministic universe of the natural philosophers (as if the universe were a machine and fate was fixed); and *freedom* was the lower plane: the human quest to be free from the deterministic

21. See Steve R. Martins, "Simon Bolivar and the True Liberator", *Cántaro Institute*. Accessed June 22, 2022, https://cantaroinstitute.org/simon-bolivar-the-true-liberator/

machinations of the universe.[22] All this to say that with the influence of Roman Catholic scholasticism and the Enlightenment's rationalism, Iberoamerican culture is nothing more than a hodgepodge of various religious syntheses without a unifying guiding principle for its progress and development. There is a lot to unpack here, but neither time, nor the context, nor the setting of this lecture allows us to dive any deeper. We will leave it at that.

## The Struggle

You will notice that I did not mention the fourth religious ground-motive, that being the *Christian* ground-motive of Creation, Fall, and Redemption. I will touch on that later, for now, however, we need to understand our relationship as Christians with public culture.

We live in interesting times given how the church has wrestled as of late with its relationship with the culture. A few generations ago, most of the church of the West was involved with nation-building, or put differently, with the cultural development of nations— whether that was the United Kingdom, Canada, the United States, etc. That is not the case anymore today. Some Christian communities have been led to believe, such as the Anabaptists, for example, that the church

---

22. See Steven R. Martins, *Towards a Christian Understanding: The Pursuit of a Christian Philosophy* (Jordan Station, ON.: Cántaro Publications, 2022), 38-39.

has no role or place in the development of public culture. Others believe that the church should forcefully Christianize public culture, drawing comparisons with Islamic efforts to Islamicize the world. And then others believe that our involvement with culture should be solely evangelistic, presupposing that the soul of man is what is solely important and not man's interactions with creation. These are only three views out of many in the Christian community, but irregardless of whether I cover all the views across the vast spectrum of opinion, from one extreme to another, the fact of reality is this: The church at large has been paralyzed in relation to its activity in public culture, and this has been due to its confusion regarding its role and calling.

Now, we do need to make a distinction between the church as an *institution* and the church as a *collective community of faith*. The church as an *institution* has its respective jurisdiction as being the administer of the gospel and its graces; it is, in other words, its own sphere. But when we speak of the church as being the *collective community of faith*, we refer to Christians involved in all the spheres of life, whether that be the family, the marketplace, academia, etc. The *institutional* church has its own sphere over which it is sovereign; the *collective* church, however, is able to operate in the spheres *outside* that of the institutional church.[23]

---

23. Abraham Kuyper, *Encyclopedia of Sacred Theology: Its Principles*, trans. J. Hendrik De Vries (New York: Charles Scribner's Sons, 1898), 587-588.

Therefore, when we speak about cultural reformation and transformation, we are referring primarily to the work belonging to the *collective community of faith*, but that work must be guided and supported by the *institutional* church. As opposed to the Catholic model of the pope exercising authority over other spheres, and therefore violating the sovereignty of the other spheres (consider, for example, the history of the papacy in the medieval era), what we instead see here are the elders of the church equipping the flock to fulfill their respective callings as God's priests, prophets, and kings in all the other spheres. I will elaborate on that threefold calling later, for now, however, it suffices to say that our objective is not to establish the church as a sovereign over other spheres—that position of sovereignty belongs to God alone—rather, to permeate each sphere with profound Christian conviction in order to reform and transform these spheres towards biblical faithfulness.

How exactly does the church do this? To be more specific, how does the church bring about *cultural renewal?* This is very different from the cultural retreatism we see today, even cultural humanism, which is the adoption of the sacred-secular divide reminiscent of the scholastic nature-grace scheme. This cultural renewal is only made possible by preaching and applying the gospel in every sphere of life. When a person's heart is *renewed* by the gospel, that renewal will extend to *everything he does* as an individual, it would thus result in the reformation of his *cultural activities*. And if this is applied collectively, we could say that the renewal of the people's hearts would result in the reformation of their cultural activities, producing a cultural reformation that would lead to *cultural transformation*. That answers the second question, as to why in that order: Because once culture has been reformed, we will see the fruits of its transformation. Before you begin to ponder where this concept of *cultural renewal* originated, let me first say that it is founded in the very nature of the gospel itself, and furthermore, it was re-discovered by the protestant reformers, and later more fully articulated and applied by the reformed Dutch statesman and theologian, Abraham Kuyper, of the late 19th and early 20th century. It was thanks to this reformational spirit and developing movement that neo-Calvinism was birthed, a strain in the Christian tradition that stands in line with Augustine, Calvin, and many others, focused not only on the reformation of the church, but on the reformation and transformation of the world, of society at large.[24]

## Understanding the Gospel

We must proceed further if we hope to better understand our role and place as Christians in the public culture, and that is by answering the next question: What is the gospel? It is a valid question, and you might be

---

24. The Neo-Calvinism Research Institute, "What is Neo-Calvinism?", *The Neo-Calvinism Research Institute*. Accessed October 26, 2021, https://www.neocalvinism.org/what-is-neo-calvinism/.

Abraham Kuyper (29 October 1837 – 8 November 1920),
*Voorzitter van de Ministerraad* (1901-1905)

surprised how few know the common answer, and how many know the common answer but not the full answer! What is the common answer we get? That the gospel is the good news of salvation in Jesus Christ for all those who turn from their sin and trust in Him as their Lord and Saviour, and that we understand this salvation not to be the result of good works, but rather entirely due to the grace of God. Is this a wrong answer? No, not at all. It captures the *heart* of the gospel, the *kernel*. Is this a biblical answer then? Yes, absolutely. But it is not the *whole* answer that the Bible provides.

Consider, for example, the writings of the apostle Paul to the Corinthian church:

> [20] But in fact Christ has been raised from the dead, the firstfruits of those who have fallen asleep. [21] For as by a man came death, by a man has come also the resurrection of the dead. [22] For as in Adam all die, so also in Christ shall all be made alive. [23] But each in his own order: Christ the firstfruits, then at his coming those who belong to Christ. [24] Then comes the end, when he delivers the kingdom to God the Father after destroying every rule and every authority and power. [25] For he must reign until he has put all his enemies under his feet. [26] The last enemy to be destroyed is death. [27] For "God has put all things in subjection under his feet." But when it says, "all things are put in subjection," it is plain that he is excepted who put all things in subjection under him. [28] When all things are subjected to him, then the Son himself will also be subjected to him who put all things in subjection under him, that God may be all in all (1 Cor. 15:20-28).

Here is a brief exposition of this Pauline text: In verses 20 to 23, Paul provides us with the gospel, that those who are in Adam are dead in their sin, but those who are in Christ are made alive, first in the spirit, later in the flesh on the day of the resurrection (v. 23). The resurrection of Jesus, the Christ, is mentioned here as the "firstfruits of those who have fallen asleep" (v. 20). This is what we understand as the common answer to the question: What is the gospel? We understand that sin is the violation of God's law; we understand that the penalty of sin is death; we understand that Adam's sin is what cast all of creation under the curse of sin, including all of his descendants; and we understand that as a result of our sin, which has caused our spiritual death—and eventual physical death—, there is coming a day where we will be judged for our sin. But for those who have repented of their sin and surrendered to the Lordship of Christ, which means dying to ourselves and renouncing our radical autonomy (or independence from God), we are forgiven, and our sins paid for in full by the death of Jesus, the Christ, which was offered up to God as a substitutionary sacrifice. And the life we have gained in Christ is the result not only of His redemptive work, but of His resurrection from the dead. This is the gospel, yes, but it is not the *whole* gospel, because Paul does not stop there.

In verses 24 to 28, Paul explains what will happen upon Christ's return: Christ will deliver the kingdom to the Father after all His enemies are destroyed, and this is not in reference to a physical war but a conflict at the worldview level; it means that all false worldviews will be shown to be false illusions, Christ will have vanquished the man who thought himself wise. There will be nothing to oppose His kingship, because the enemy will have been utterly defeated. But this will not be a sudden event, such as in "the blink of an eye." His return will certainly be in the blink of an eye, but not His *victory*, we will see instead the victory of Christ progressing with the passing of time. We know this because Paul says this, that Christ is reigning in the present tense (v. 25), and that while He reigns, all His enemies are being put under His feet, and the last enemy to be destroyed, before He hands the kingdom to the Father, is death (v. 26). We understand, of course, that death will not be vanquished until He returns in bodily form, and so for that reason, death is the last enemy. But that is not to say that Christ's reign is limited until His return, because Paul also says that all things have already been made subject to Him (v. 27). We could put it this way: Jesus Christ is Lord over all creation, everything is subject to His Lordship, and presently Christ is bringing order to a fallen creation, through both renewal and judgment. And the day that He returns will mark the destruction of the final enemy, death, and the proclamation of His total triumph. Those who remain in their sin will face the final judgment, but those who were captured by His grace will experience full renewal and a new creation, with Jesus as the sovereign King.

How then do we articulate this gospel *totally*? That *Jesus Christ is Lord over all creation, bringing all things subject to Himself, and that salvation is found in Him by the grace of God alone.* This short answer captures the good news of (i) Christ's reign on the throne as Lord, and (ii) the salvation He offers to all who repent (turn from their sin) and believe (surrender to Him). With this understanding of the gospel, we can now see that the gospel is not confined to one's spirituality, but is extensive and expansive, encompassing every facet, every sphere, of human life.

**Understanding Culture**

That now brings us to the next question, What is culture? Culture is the inevitable result of man's cultivation of creation.[25] If we think of a tree, for example, we are referring to creation. But when man cuts down that tree for building a house, or for producing an axe, his interaction with creation results in the creation of culture. The same could be said of sound. Sound is a part of God's creation, but what if man were to produce sound and order it in such a way that it becomes music? Again, we see man's interaction with creation producing culture. The sound of a tree falling is not the same as the sound of the piano when someone plays Beethoven or Mozart. What about tomatoes? A tomato is a part of God's creation, but when man harvests the tomato and uses it to make tomato sauce for a pizza, we see again the creation of culture. There is a clear distinction between what is God's creation, and what is culture. There can be no culture without God's creation, but there *can* be creation without culture. Whenever man interacts with God's creation, however, he *inevitably* creates culture.

While that certainly helps us, we may still be wrestling with understanding "culture". What exactly is

---

25. See P. Andrew Sandlin, *Christian Culture: An Introduction* (CA.: Center for Cultural Leadership, 2013).

*"The Rebuilding of the Temple"*, from the Book of Ezra, by Gustave Doré (1832-1883)

culture? We can use the illustration of an apple to understand the anatomy of culture. The skin of an apple is like the behaviours and customs of the people, the flesh of the apple beneath the skin is like the values of the people, and the core of the apple is like the beliefs of the people. Beliefs (or worldviews) lead to the formation of values, and values lead to the formation of behaviours and customs. Whether cultural retreatists like it or not, everyone is involved in creating culture, and because everyone has a religious ground-motive (or a base religious motive), because everyone has a *worldview* by which they interpret the world around them, then that ultimately means two things: (i) we cannot escape culture, and (ii) culture is not secular, or irreligious. If culture building is, therefore, inescapable, and if it is religious by nature, because man is a religious being after all, then culture must be understood as a form of worship either towards God (true worship) or towards some creational aspect (idolatry and apostasy). If we look at, for example, the Middle East, we will find Islamic culture. If we look at Israel, we will find Jewish culture. If we look at Canada, we will find a secular humanistic culture, which is just as religious as the other two because man has simply substituted God for man, what we would call the "deification of man in an implicit manner." As we consider these examples, there is, therefore, another way of defining culture, not solely as the product of man's interaction with creation, but as: *the religion of the people externalized.*

## Understanding the Relation between Gospel and Culture

That now leaves us with the last question. Before we can proceed to what steps we can take toward building a reformation movement, we must ask: What is the relationship between gospel and culture? I touched on this briefly when discussing cultural renewal, but more specifically, I am going to be discussing the cultural mandate, how the cultural mandate is renewed in the Great Commission, and re-visiting our threefold calling as prophet, priest, and king.

In the beginning, when God created Adam and Eve, He placed them in the garden, and having placed all of creation under their authority (Gen. 1:26-28), subject to God of course, they were tasked with tending it (Gen. 2:15). What did this mean? What did it mean to exercise dominion over the earth? What did it mean to tend the garden? Theologians have interpreted this as the *cultural mandate*, which can be expressed as the call of man to cultivate creation into a godly civilization.[26] How was man to do this? Well, both Adam and Eve had the threefold office of prophet, priest, and king (in Eve's case, queen).[27] To be a prophet was to interpret creation (or reality) according to God's revelation; to be a priest was to dedicate creation unto God as a form of worship; and to be a king was to govern creation subject to God and His law.[28] This was how man was to fulfill the cultural mandate. However, when man fell by his original sin, it became impossible for man to fulfill the cultural mandate. How could sinful man cultivate creation into a godly civilization? His sin would taint the whole initiative. This did not, however, negate his threefold calling. In his sin, mankind became his

26. See Joseph Boot, *Gospel Culture: Living in God's Kingdom*, Cornerstones Vol. 1 (Toronto, ON.: Ezra Press, 2016).

27. See Herman Bavinck, "The Origin, Essence and Purpose of Man," in *Selected Shorter Works of Herman Bavinck*, ed. John Hendryx (West Linn, OR.: Monergism Books, 2015).

28. See Steven R. Martins, "The Threefold Office of Man", in *La Fuente: Iberoamerican Journal for Christian Worldview*, Vol. 2, No. 1, 2022 (Cántaro Publications), 15-26.

Fourth century BC, red figure pottery. The scene on this Attic vase depicts a myth-ical garden; the Garden of the Hesperides, which is widely interpreted as the Ancient Greek version of the Garden of Eden.

own prophet, priest, and king; interpreting creation (or reality) according to his own thoughts, dedicating cre-ation unto himself as a form of worship, and govern-ing according to his whims and desires. The reason this calling was not negated is because it is rooted in our nature, we were created to fulfill this function rightly before God, and it would not be until the fulfillment of Christ's redemptive work that this mandate would then be renewed. How was this renewed? If the first Adam had failed, the second Adam would not, that be-ing Jesus, the Christ. Jesus is the true prophet, priest, and king, and it is only by His *power* that the cultural mandate can be fulfilled. Within what context can this mandate be fulfilled? Within the Great Commission, as we read in Matthew 28:18-20:

> ... "All authority in heaven and on earth has been given to me. Go therefore and make disciples of all nations, baptizing them in the name of the Father and of the Son and of the Holy Spirit, teaching them to observe all that I have commanded you. And behold, I am with you always, to the end of the age."

In Christ, therefore, we are God's prophets, priests, and kings, and being such, we are tasked with fulfilling the cultural mandate within the context of the Great Commission: *to cultivate creation into a godly civilization by means of gospel renewal.*

This is where Dooyeweerd's fourth ground-motive comes into view, of *Creation-Fall-Redemption.* Our cultural activity is not meaningless, it is based on the presupposition of the foundational significance and importance of the biblical metanarrative for understanding reality. This philosophical framework, introduced and developed by Dooyeweerd, posits three periods of radical cosmic change: Creation, Fall, and Redemption.[29] We are not, of course, in the period of Creation, and while we still see the fallen condition of creation today, we are not in the period of the Fall, instead, we are in the period of Redemption, where Christ, by His Spirit and through His church, is redeeming all of creation, beginning with the human heart and extending to man's cultural activities. We operate according to that

---

29. See Dooyeweerd, *Roots of Western Culture.*

conviction, rejecting the dualisms of the other philosophical schemas, affirming the Lordship of Christ over all creation, and remaining faithful to the unified revelation of God in both creation and Scripture.

## The Steps Towards Reformation

Now that we have an understanding as to why there must be a reformation and transformation of Iberoamerican (and Western) culture, and now that we also have an understanding of the gospel, culture, and our place in it, we can now look at the steps we can take towards building a reformation movement. What I am about to present to you is a three-stage model that begins with the institutional church and extends to the collective community of faith (remember the distinction).

The first stage can be called "The Basics", which consists of the constitutional church fulfilling its threefold mission. Systematic theologians will almost all agree that the church exists to glorify God through (i) evangelism, (ii) discipleship, and (iii) worship. To break that down a bit further, evangelism involves the proclamation of the gospel for the salvation of the lost; discipleship involves the discipling of believers in the Word of God—and, if done rightly, will produce disciple-making disciples; and worship involves the worship of God in every facet and sphere of life. You would be surprised how few churches, either in the Western Anglosphere, or in Ibero-America, commit themselves to fulfilling this threefold mission. I often talk about how the *whole* gospel, the *totality* of the gospel, is truncated to soteriology *only*, but, in fact, there are churches that are even losing sight of *that*, and therefore failing in their most basic calling. If a church cannot fulfill its basic calling, then it cannot proceed forward and participate meaningfully in a reformation movement.

The second stage can be called "The Intermediary", and this presupposes that the church has mastered the first stage, "The Basics." In "The Intermediary" stage, the institutional church builds upon the foundation of the first stage by providing specialized training relating to man's relationship to the world in all societal spheres. In order to achieve this well, we need to understand the cultural activity of man as presupposing three relationships: (i) his relationship to God; (ii) his relationship to fellow man; and (iii) his relationship to creation (whatever is beneath man). If man's relationship to God is restored through the gospel, then he can experience a restoration of the other two relationships evidenced by how he lives in the different spheres of life. It should be noted that this specialized training goes beyond seeing man as a traditional missionary, as we see depicted in the first stage, and is more focused on cultivating Christians for all the life spheres that they will engage in. For example, at this stage, the church will be focused on cultivating, through discipleship, Christian fathers and mothers, Christian businessmen, Christian politicians, Christian lawyers, Christian philosophers,

Christian psychologists, Christian biologists, Christian sociologists, Christian teachers, etc. It is not simply a matter of being a Christian and having a profession or a calling, we cannot adopt the false sacred-secular divide of our fallen culture, it is instead to have a *Christian* understanding of parenthood, business, politics, law, philosophy, science, and education. To put it more simply, this stage has more to do with training Christians as missionaries, not in the traditional sense, but in a *contextualized* sense, where they can pay tribute to the Lordship of Christ through their respective vocations.

Of course, what is specialized training without specialized mobilization? That brings us to the third stage, and this is where we ought to see a transition from the institutional church to the collective community of faith, because it now involves mobilizing specialized missionaries to other spheres. This third and final stage can be called "The Advanced", as it presupposes a collective church that has come from an institutional church which has mastered the first and second stages. This is the stage where we get into the formation of Christian reformational political parties, Christian reformational academies (from schools to Universities, not merely Seminaries), Christian reformational labour unions, Christian reformational laboratories, etc.. It is called the advanced stage for a reason, because though we know where we need to go, we have not been able to get there. And the best example of this in recent history was what we saw in Kuyper's day, who was not only

# THE BASIC
# THE INTERMEDIATE
# THE ADVANCED

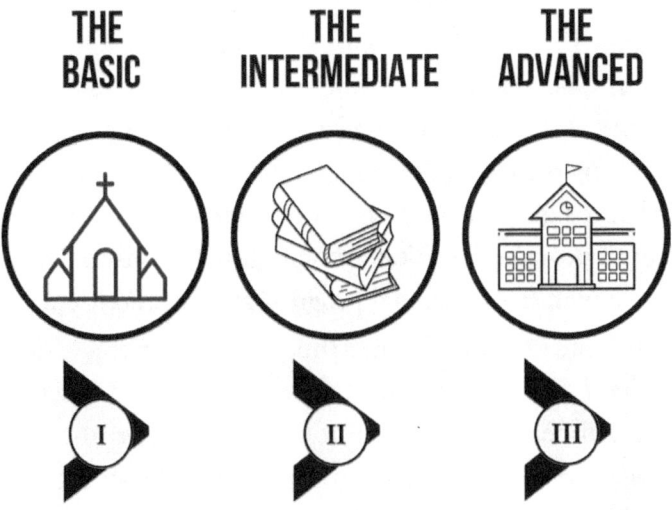

involved with a Christian reformational political party, but also founded the Free University of Amsterdam (alas, what that institution has become is a far cry from what it used to be). We do not have anything like this in Ibero-America (or the West), but we should, we can! The potential is there, the building blocks are there, I would go as far as to say that the conditions are actually more favourable for Ibero-America to see this reformation realized than the Anglosphere today—there is less cultural resistance in your Iberoamerican context, for example. What we need, however, is a spirit of humility, a spirit of unity, and a strong conviction to see this through until the very end, that being, when Christ returns. This is not the work of a single church, or of a small group of churches, but rather of the church throughout Ibero-America (the same goes for the West). Perhaps it begins in El Salvador, perhaps it begins in Guatemala, or in the Dominican Republic, or in Colombia, it does not matter where it begins, as long as it begins, and as long as steps are taken towards drawing the rest of the church into this movement. And what a sight it would be if the Iberoamerican church could provoke the Western church to jealousy with its missional, reformational progress and advancement.

Time is short, let me thus summarize this three-stage model prior to our departure. We could describe the different stages in the following manner: the first stage, "The Basics", concerns foundational training and mobilization; the second stage, "The Intermediary", concerns specialized training; and the third stage, "The Advanced", concerns specialized mobilization. It begins with the institutional church, because it is the church that trains and mobilizes; and it extends to the collective church, because it is Christians in all facets and spheres of life who will, by the power, grace, and the will of God, bring all things in subjection to the Lordship of Christ. Yes, Christ is already Lord. Yes, all things are subject to Him. But they do not yet appear as subject to His reign, and that is where we come in, as His missional agents, to proclaim and apply the *whole* gospel, to bear witness of the "gospel renewal" all around us, up until that final day, when the triumph of Christ is made evident to all. *Maranatha!* Come Lord Jesus! We yearn for that final restoration. But in the meantime, to the harvest fellow believers! For we are short of labourers, and the task before us is great (Matt. 9:37; Luke 10:2).

# III

# THE LENS BY WHICH WE SEE THE WORLD

**Date:** April 29, 2023

**Context:** Cántaro Institute 2023 Niagara Conference

**Setting:** Faith Life & Centre, Brock University, St. Catharines, Ontario, Canada

## Introductory Remarks

THANK YOU, and grace and peace to you all.

Let me begin with a question to help break the ice and establish our context: How many of you here have watched the movie *Book of Eli* (2010) starring Denzel Washington? It is not characterized as a family-friendly movie, so I would not be surprised if only *few* have watched it. The movie is about the preservation of the Bible in a fictional, post-apocalyptic world. Washington plays this character named "Eli", who guards what is believed to be the last copy of the Bible, and it happens to be in Braille.[1] Over the course of the film, we find out that Eli had committed the whole Bible to memory, so when the book is stolen from him in the third act, the Bible is not really lost. It is instead passed on orally to someone else, with the intention of ensuring its preservation. Throughout the story we are brought through the challenges and risks that Eli has to go undergo, but the movie also illustrates the significance of the Bible itself. Within the context of the film, it is almost as if civilization *depends* on this book. As if the reformation and/or reconstitution of society *hinges* upon this book. Well, contrary to what skeptics might think, there is a profound truth to that.

In addition to being the top-selling book in the world—and over the course of all literary history—, the Bible is also the most *printed* book in the world (consider, for example, how many copies have been produced for international missions). To give you a bit of an idea, in 2015 the Guinness Book of World Records estimated that more than 5 *billion* copies of the Bible had been printed. There is not a single book in the history of mankind that comes close to that number. The Bible is of such significance, it is of such power, that—as per Steve and Jackie Green, the founders of the Museum of the Bible—it has impacted and given

---

1.  A linguistic system of raised dots that represent the letters of the alphabet, developed in the early 1800s so that the visually impaired could read.

*The Book of Eli* (Warner Bros.). Rated R.
Not recommended for minors.

shape to much of Western human history:

> Indeed, the Bible has stirred up controversies that have
> affected empires. People have been burned alive in their
> attempt to translate it for the common person… it's
> been the source behind those who worked in England
> to abolish the slave trade… It has changed cultural
> views on women, children, and the oppressed. It guided
> the first Christians in the first century toward a morality
> unseen in the Roman world. It moved a young monk
> to call out injustices in the church, an act which led to
> the Protestant Reformation. It has inspired artists such
> as Bach and Rembrandt. It was the guiding light for

world-changing intellectuals like Blaise Pascal. Its printing was one of the most significant events of the last millennia.[2]

Could we honestly expect *anything less* from the inspired, *inscripturated*, Word of God?

## What is the "Word of God"?

For those of us who come from a Christian background, the answer to the question "What is the Word of God?" might be a bit redundant. But for those in our midst who do not espouse a Christian worldview, the "Word of God" is the *entirety* of the Old and New Testaments. You see, the Bible is a collection of 66 books: 39 books in the Old Testament, and 27 books in the New Testament. The word "Bible" is derived from the Greek word *biblia* (for "books"), which, though plural, came to be used as a singular noun, and stands for the collection that we as Christians acknowledge to be the *Word of God*. This idea, or concept, of collecting these holy writings into a formal collection developed in early Hebrew-Christian thought. The prophet Daniel, for example, spoke of the prophetic writings, sometime in the 6th century BC, as "the books" (Dan. 9:2). The writer of 1 Maccabees referred to the Old Testament corpus, in the 2nd century BC, as "the holy books" (12:9). Jesus referred to the Old Testament books as "the Scriptures"

---

2.　Steve and Jackie Green, *This Dangerous Book: How the Bible Has Shaped Our World and Why It Still Matters Today* (Grand Rapids, MI.: Zondervan, 2017), 15.

THE LENS BY WHICH WE SEE THE WORLD

in Matthew 21:42. And the apostle Paul referred to them as "the holy Scriptures" in Romans 1:2, likewise with Jesus on the AD side of history. Altogether, the entirety of this corpus of literature is "inspired", as in "God-breathed" (for that is what is meant by the term), not because the church declared it to be, but because (i) the Scriptures declare themselves to be (2 Tim. 3:16-17), and (ii) because its propositions can be verified as being true.

Where do the Scriptures declare themselves to be God's "breathed-out" Word? Consider 2 Timothy 3:16-17:

> All Scripture is breathed out by God and profitable for teaching, for reproof, for correction, and for training in righteousness, that the man of God may be complete, equipped for every good work.

A noteworthy fact on the Word's inspiration, and this was originally presented by the late apologist Greg L. Bahnsen (1948-1995) in one of his lectures: the Bible is the *only holy or religious book that self-testifies of its inspiration*. And as an inspired text, it is both infallible (it cannot be wrong in what it teaches) and inerrant (it is free of all errors) because God Himself is infallible and inerrant. Now, for some of you, that may have been a bit of a review of our most basic Bibliology, and I am sure that you did not come to us for that this morning. But for those amongst us who are inquiring about our Christian faith, it was necessary. Now let us go deeper into the nature and role of the Word of God, but in a manner of thinking that I am sure you may not have considered before.

## The Bible as God's THESIS

The Bible is more than just a collection of religious books. It is more than just a historical and cultural treasure trove of literary antiquities. It is more than a highly revered book for a religious community that calls itself Christian (and whatever branches within Christianity you could possibly imagine). Given that the Bible is the inspired WORD of God—note the singular here, underlying all the diversity of the Scriptures is "the unity of the Word of God"—, and given that there are no sure grounds in our human methods (this is because we are fallen and limited beings, which I will expand on later), the Word of God is the only firm foundation for *all* of human life.[3] Not just for the Christian, not just for the supposedly "religious" (as if religious neutrality was ever a thing), not just for the reader, but for *all of humanity*, for *all of civilization*. I can put it another way: the Bible is the *only lens by which we can see the world for what it truly is*, and *by which we can order our lives*.

Since the Enlightenment—though we do see traces of this in the patristic age (the age of the church fathers) with the meddling of Greek philosophic thought—

---

3. H. Evan Runner, *The Relation of the Bible to Learning* (Jordan Station, ON.: Paideia Press, 2023), 22-23.

there has been an increasing tendency to approach the Word with our own presuppositions, presuppositions which are contrary to the Word. And while this is true of fallen man ever since the Word was first progressively revealed, it has become more *systematized* and *pervasive*. And in such circumstances, the meaning of the Word inevitably becomes lost to the reader. William Tyndale, the English Bible translator of the 16th century, for example, once wrote that the Christian scholars of his age were pumped full of so much scholastic/heathen thought and elaborate humanistic methods that when the time came to read the Scriptures, it was like a wall had been built around it and its meaning had been locked away.[4] The truth is, it is not *we* who come with our understanding to the Word of God. It does not work that way. As the late American Christian philosopher H. Evan Runner (1916-2002) had put it:

---

4. Tyndale had this to say, "In the Universities they have ordained that no man shall look at the scripture, until he be noselled in heathen learning eight or nine years, and armed with false principles; with which he is clean shut out of the understanding of scripture... And then, when they be admitted to study divinity, because the scripture is locked up with such false expositions, and with false principles of natural philosophy, that they cannot enter in, they go about the outside, and dispute all their lives about words and vain opinions...." See William Tyndale, "Practice of Prelates," in *Expositions and Notes on Sundry Portions of the Holy Scriptures together with the Practice of Prelates*, ed. H. Walker (1849; repr., Cambridge: Cambridge University Press, 1968), 291.

William Tyndale (c. 1494–c. 1536) was martyred for his protestant convictions
and for having translated the Bible into English.

…it is the WORD, which is the POWER of God, that
comes to our hearts and opens our eyes so that we may
understand the singleness of meaning of all the many
Scriptures.[5]

As the *inspired* Word of God, the Bible is therefore
authoritative; and being authoritative, it supersedes
our understanding, it supersedes our presuppositions.
Vishal Mangalwadi, who is scheduled to speak in the
last session of our conference, often uses an originally
Buddhist illustration of five blind men and an elephant
as it relates to *knowing* the truth. I trust he does not
mind me borrowing it this morning. In the illustration,
five blind men all touch a part of an elephant and try to

---

5.    Runner, *The Relation of the Bible to Learning*, 23.

define what an elephant is. It appears as if they all have a *piece* of the truth, but they cannot have the truth, because they are all blind. The person who *really* has the truth is the sixth person who is *not* blind, the only possible person who could tell it just as it is (how convenient that this sixth person is never mentioned). We are *limited* beings, incapable of grasping the total cosmic scale of our reality. And the effect of our sin further hampers our efforts, causing us to suppress the truth. The apostle Paul, in his letter to Rome, wrote that "...the wrath of God is revealed from heaven against all ungodliness and unrighteousness of men, *who by their unrighteousness suppress the truth*" (1:18). To translate the latter portion of that verse into more understandable terms, Paul is saying that our human nature, tainted by sin, causes us to *suppress* the truth. We put on our own blindfolds, and thus we cannot possibly arrive at the truth ourselves. It is for that reason that the truth must come to us. And it has, in the form of the Son of God, Jesus, the Christ, who is Himself the Word—as well as in the form of God's inscripturated revelation, the Word, which in the first place *reveals* the Christ to us.

And what *does* this Word reveal? **Firstly**, it reveals who God is. Consider, for example, that Genesis 1:1 does not begin with mankind, nor with creation. No, it begins with God: "In the beginning, GOD..." The God of the Bible is not one of many. He is not an *impersonal* being or some *abstract* entity. He is the sole

Sovereign, personal, Creator God. *Secondly*, it reveals who man is, *what* he is and *who* he is meant to be (and of course, I am including women in that as well). And *thirdly*, it reveals the will of God for man, man's *purpose*, his intended *function*, his created *destiny*. And the content of that revelation not only informs us as to the state of things: (i) as to what is; and (ii) what is not; and (iii) where things stand; it also serves as a guiding and governing principle as to how we ought to live. And this is laid out in the Word as it relates to our threefold relationships, as to[6]

1. how we ought to live in relation to God;
2. how we ought to live in relation to one another; and
3. how we ought to live in relation to creation.

But the content of this revelation is not static, nor abstract. It is instead laid out over the course of a historical narrative, a schema that begins with Creation, then followed by the Fall, and ending with Redemption, which, we should note, has not yet been made fully manifest. In the Word we learned of the *original* state of things, what happened that *altered* the state of things, and what was done to *remedy* the state of things.[7] With this we come to understand the world

---

6. D. F. M. Strauss, *Being Human in God's World* (Jordan Station, ON.: Paideia Press, 2020), 38-39.

7. See Steven R. Martins: *The Gospel (Foundations, Vol. I)* (Jordan Station, ON.: Cántaro Publications, 2023).

H. Evan Runner (1916 –2002), portrait from
*Hearing and Doing* (Wedge Pub., 1979)

as not being purposeless, but rather, as having an overarching story, a meta-narrative. This is what led Runner to refer to the Word as the divine THESIS, in the
sense that the Word of God posits the truth, and it
was the truth that first and always was. After which
followed distortions of the truth as a result of the Fall.
But with the provision of the Word unto men, that is,
the inscripturated revelation of God, the Word is to be
regarded as the *republication* of the divine THESIS.[8] To

8.  Runner, *The Relation of the Bible to Learning*, 45, 49. See
    also Louis Berkhof, *Introductory Volume to Systematic Theol-*
    *ogy* (Grand Rapids, MI.: Wm. B. Eerdmans Publishing Co.,

use Runner's words:

> The Word of God is God's THESIS, the first and only True Statement, by which the nature of our life in the world is elucidated and its way (thus) directed.[9]

What do we mean by truth, as it relates to its revelation in the Word? We mean the whole of reality in its central religious meaning. You see, the presuppositions, or the worldview provided by Scripture provides for us the *thinkware* for a right understanding of all things as it relates to God, ourselves, and our place in this world. It is the lens by which we see the world: the lens by which we interpret the *facts* of our world. For those unfamiliar with the concept of *worldview*, it can be defined as:

> A network of presuppositions (which are not verified by the procedures of natural science) regarding reality (metaphysics), knowing (epistemology), and conduct (ethics) in terms of which every element of human experience is related and interpreted.[10]

Everyone has a worldview, a set of presuppositions (or what we believe to be true), by which we interpret human experience. But not every worldview succeeds

---

1932), 60.

9. Ibid., 50.

10. Gary DeMar, ed., *Pushing the Antithesis: The Apologetic Methodology of Greg L. Bahnsen* (Powder Springs, GA.: American Vision Press, 2010), 42-43.

in providing man with a proper understanding. In other words, not every worldview provides man with truth. As a matter of fact, the claim of Scripture is that nothing can be *truly* known outside of itself. Where do we see that? Well, for starters, Proverbs 9:10, "The fear of the Lord is *the beginning of wisdom*, and the knowledge of the Holy One is *insight (or understanding)*." That's not some fortune-cookie wisdom, or some devotional tidbit. According to the Hebrew understanding of "wisdom", particularly as it relates to wisdom literature, wisdom encompasses a *right understanding* of all things. And such wisdom is unattainable outside of the means by which God has made it known to the world. Following this biblical principle or truth claim, the late apologist Cornelius Van Til carried it out to its inevitable implication. In his tract titled *Why I Believe in God*, he writes:

> Now in fact, I feel that the whole of history and civilization would be unintelligible to me if it were not for my belief in God. So true is this, that I propose to argue that unless God is back of everything, you cannot find meaning in anything.[11]

Put differently, we might say that by virtue of the fact that we are God's creation, and that we live in God's world, and that we were created to live in, and

---

11. Cornelius Van Til, *Why I Believe in God* (Philadelphia: Committee on Christian Education of the Orthodox Presbyterian Church, n.d.), 3.

to function in this world, we cannot then possibly arrive at any *true* knowledge without first presupposing the God who created us. And that is not to say that we cannot arrive at *any* knowledge, but that we cannot *truly* know anything outside of the worldview, or presuppositions, provided to us by the divinely inspired Word. Now, you might say, "Hold on a sec, what about the simple facts of life?" The statement, for example, that 2 + 2 = 4, that remains true for everyone does it not? Whether it might be mathematics, physics, logic, etc., much of what we see, observe, and verify to be true in the natural world, all of this remains the same across the board.[12] That does not change. If that were not so, how could we possibly have any social exchange with others? It is a valid question. Van Til answered that question by making a distinction between knowing and *truly* knowing.[13] The naturalist, for example, can agree with the Christian that 2 + 2 = 4, but can he make sense of that mathematical formulation? Can he make sense of mathematical law in a universe that is devoid of a Law-Giver? That is, in a universe that is governed by random causality given that its point of origin is random probability itself? The Christian does not have that dilemma. He has the answer to those questions, because he *can* make sense of the intelligibil-

---

12. Runner, *The Relation of the Bible to Learning*, 10.

13. See Cornelius Van Til, *Christian Apologetics*, second edition, ed. William Edgar (Phillipsburg, NJ.: P&R Publishing, 2003).

ity of reality—it is what some philosophers have called the *predication of reality*. Those answers ultimately lie in the God who has revealed Himself through creation and His Word. And as it relates to creation, I do not just mean the surface level of what Paul refers to in Romans 1:19-20, in which he writes:

> For what can be known about God is plain to them, because God has shown it to them. For his invisible attributes, namely, his eternal power and divine nature, have been clearly perceived, ever since the creation of the world, in the things that have been made. So they are without excuse.

It is true that everyone marvels at the sun, the moon, and the stars—not that long ago several were marveling at the aurora borealis that had extended so far South. But what I am referring to is creation at a much *deeper* level, at a much more *sophisticated* level. Drawing back the curtains to see backstage so to speak. "Mathematical laws, physical laws, laws for organic growth, laws of thought, economic and aesthetic laws, etc.", as Runner puts it, every law in our creational reality is "every word of God by which He has subjected creation to His Will or Rule. Law is thus nothing other than the Will of the sovereign God for His creation."[14] Look at the whole creation narrative, look at the two opening chapters of Genesis. It is not possible to have a right understanding of reality, a reality that we can make sense of, if we do

---

14. Runner, *The Relation of the Bible to Learning*, 30.

not first understand our reality in light of the Sovereign Creator God. And to understand such, we need the *inscripturated* Word of God. We need the *republication* of God's revelation as it concerns the truth of all things.[15] And that republication was necessary, in part because of the *noetic* effects of our sin (the influence of sin upon the human mind). Though also, in part, because God so willed to reveal to us the means of redemption of all things.

This audacious claim—and it is an audacious claim, it is a claim that Scripture can certainly make given that it is in fact the *inspired* Word of God—that we cannot *truly* know anything outside of the worldview or presuppositions provided to us by Scripture, may lead us to question our learning process as it relates to the varied disciplines. How can we *truly* know anything in the disciplines? How much can the disciplines inform our understanding of the world, if at all? The answer, of course, is not *irrationalism*. One might be tempted to accuse us of this. And no, the answer is not found in *Rationalist* thought either.

We have all been culturally conditioned—and this due in part to the influence of Enlightenment or Rationalist thought—to think that the disciplines or the sciences can be viewed and understood as abstract or

---

15. Cornelius Van Til, *An Introduction to Systematic Theology: Prolegomena and the Doctrines of Revelation, Scripture, and God*, ed. William Edgar (Phillipsburg, NJ.: P&R Publishing, 2007), 225.

independent entities. And for many these entities have become *absolutized* or *deified* (I will address that shortly). But to partition away the disciplines or sciences from their central unity of meaning is to take away what makes those fields meaningful and intelligible. The late Dutch scholar Vollenhoven, as well as Van Til, argued that to understand the varied disciplines or sciences, one must see them "in the revealing light of the Word of God."[16] It is not to say that the Word serves as a textbook guide to the disciplines (no one would say that the Bible speaks to us about chemistry or physics directly), but rather, that the Word provides us with the intellectual parameters by which we can *rightly* understand the disciplines.[17] To put it another way, it is when we understand what the Word of God is and the function that it ought to occupy in our lives that we can then have a biblical, Christian worldview by which we can see the world and by which we can order our lives.[18]

An excellent illustration of this truth was provided by R.B. Kuiper, former chairman of the faculty of Westminster Theological Seminary and former president of Calvin College. Initially, the illustration was meant to convey the function of man within the creat-

---

16. See Runner, *The Relation of the Bible to Learning*, 11.

17. See Steven R. Martins, *Apologetics: Studies in Biblical Apologetics for a Christian Worldview* (Jordan Station, ON.: Cántaro Publications, 2020) 144.

18. Runner, *The Relation of the Bible to Learning*, 19.

ed order that he had been created for. But, it also serves to explain how we can only make sense of reality within the Christian worldview, within the truth itself. The illustration consists of an elderly woman, a friend she visits, and a fish. It goes as follows:

> [An] old lady… went to visit a friend. When her hostess disappeared into her kitchen for a few minutes, this peculiar lady got up out of her chair and, walking about the salon, found a bowl of tropical fish behind the grand piano. In a sudden inspiration she reached her hand into the bowl, lifted out one of the fish and dropped it tenderly onto the rich carpeting that covered the floor. As she did so she muttered to herself, "Wicked old woman, keeping you shut up in that little old bowl! I'm going to give you the freedom of this whole salon." Of course, the fish promptly proceeded to expire. Why? Because it had been removed from that law-area for which it had been created.[19]

---

19. Cited in Ibid., 38.

This is the case with fallen man. Outside of the worldview or presuppositions provided by the Word, he can make *no sense* of our world; he can make no sense of the *intelligibility* of our world. The necessary preconditions for intelligibility, referred to by Van Til and Bahnsen, are forfeit the moment man steps outside of the truth and into his imaginary perspective (or distortion) of the cosmos. And his failure to make sense of reality does not begin with creation outside of himself, but with his own selfhood. The self is plunged into obscurity, having been yanked from its true religious context. You see, man cannot truly be man, he cannot *truly* know himself, or the world in which he lives, or the God behind the world, if he is not within the parameters, the presuppositions, the *worldview*, provided by the inspired Word. And what is most telling is that, though the natural man has concocted his own antithetical worldview, he does not *live* according to his own worldview, not consistently that is.[20] The run-off-the-mill naturalist, for example, who happens to believe in a non-theistic universe, should in theory believe in the fluidity of the world, an ever-changing reality, being the inevitable product of random chance. In such a world, there can be no such thing as uniformity. There can be no fixed laws. One moment the law of gravity applies, the next it no longer does. One day 2 + 2 = 4, but the next it no longer does. But the nat-

---

20. Frame, *A History of Western Philosophy and Theology* (Phillipsburg, NJ.: P&R Publishing, 2015), 152.

uralist does not actually *expect* that, he does not *anticipate* that, because in his living and thinking he *anticipates* that which is contrary to what his presuppositions imply. The natural man, in his antithetical worldview, is a walking and talking contradiction. He believes in an altogether different worldview than what is actually revealed by the Word to be true, but he lives and breathes in such a way that presupposes the God of the Bible, that presupposes that very truth. There is a lot more depth here that I would love to go into, but for the sake of time, I would encourage you to check out Bahnsen's book *Pushing the Antithesis*, as well as my own book titled *Apologetics*. For now, it is enough for me to say that the natural man can do little else than borrow the capital, the grounds, of the Christian worldview, for his own living and thinking.

## Man's Proposed ANTITHESIS

Now, I have said much about the Word being the divine THESIS, as it being the only lens by which we can see the world and by which we can order our lives. But how do we make sense of alternative philosophies and worldviews? How do we make sense of the ANTITHESIS? Well, we can begin by first asking what it is that we mean by ANTITHESIS? It is not meant in a subjective sense, as in say the distinctions that may exist between me and you. It is also not meant in the sense of two people groups, those of the City (or Kingdom) of God and those of the city of man, to use St.

Augustine's terminology for *the people of God* and *the people of the world*. The definition for ANTITHESIS is provided by Runner as

> the difference of response to the Word of God, which, coming into the world as a revealing light for our life (Ps. 119:105), effectuates with the sovereignty of its Divine Author an abiding line of division between ways obedient and disobedient (cf. Psalm 1; Prov. 1 and 2).[21]

In other words, ANTITHESIS is the product and result of our disobedience to God's Word. It is what stands in opposition to the truth revealed in God's unified revelation, that being His creation and His inscripturated Word. It is, to put it simply, a systematic and religious distortion of the Creation-Order. And the ANTITHESIS is in fact quite varied.[22] The individual who rejects the revealed truth of God for the lie will still live subject to the created order that God established, and by virtue of the fact that he cannot escape God's world, he is haunted by the truth of who God is and what he (or she) as a created individual was meant to be. It does not matter, at the end of the day, how much one claims to be a secularist or a naturalist, even in a post-Fall context, we are still, by nature, religious beings. And because man is inescapably a religious being, he cannot help but replace God with some absolutized aspect of creation. It is the only place he can turn

---

21. Runner, *The Relation of the Bible to Learning*, 17.

22. Ibid., 73.

"Ananke" as represented by a modern illustration
(personification) of Plato's *Republic*.

to, though it always proves to be a dead end.

The ancient Greeks, for example, who had their own pantheon and mythology, believed that their god-like beings were ultimately subject to a more ultimate law of Necessity, what they called *Ananke*. It was a necessary "form" of some sort that determined everything. And as an abstract concept, it became absolutized, *deified*. As Runner laid it out, "In the realistic philosophy of Plato to such absolute, abstract law-essences—e.g. "the beautiful itself," "the just itself," etc.—hold for the gods as well as for men."[23] It has always been the tendency of fallen man to substitute the true God with some absolutized aspect of created reality.

---

23. Runner, *The Relation of the Bible to Learning*, 31.

Paul, again in his first chapter to the Romans, explains that man can worship only one of two things: the Creator, or the creation; there is no third object of worship. Upon this revealed truth, Christian scholar Peter Jones, in his book *One or Two*, explains that there can only then exist two types of worldviews: *Oneism* and *Twoism*.[24] In a Oneist worldview, man worships some aspect of creation, it is a worldview in which there exists no distinction between Creator and creation. And within such a worldview, distinctions cannot therefore exist, given that the ultimate distinction that is required for the intelligibility of reality is not maintained. It fails, in other words, to meet the preconditions of intelligibility. And it is specifically the *Oneist* worldview—which encompasses *every* worldview contrary to that of the Word—that is the ANTITHESIS. The Twoist worldview, on the other hand, is that worldview that *does* preserve that Creator-creation distinction, it *does* meet the preconditions of intelligibility. It is nothing other than the divine THESIS, the inspired Word of God.

What might be an example of the ANTITHESIS? Well, returning to man's struggle with understanding himself apart from the Word, consider his attempts to define himself: Over the course of history, man has never independently arrived at a point of satisfaction as it relates to the meaning of the self. There really has

---

24. See Peter Jones, *Gospel Truth, Pagan Lies: Can You Tell the Difference?* (Escondido, CA.: Main Entry Editions, 2004).

been no universal consensus. The tendency has always been to absolutize a certain aspect of God's creation, and we see this for example with rationalism, materialism, aestheticism, organicism, technicism, etc., all the —isms that have sought to provide a *totality-view* of man. Within rationalism, which by the way is an absolutization (and deification) of our analytical capacity, man is conceived of as a rational being; within materialism, as a material organization; within technicism, as a technical being.[25] In the end, after much thought and debate, the question remains, "Just what is man"? They certainly grasp something of the truth, like the blind men standing by the elephant, but they distort it, exaggerate it. We recognize ourselves to be rational beings of course, but clearly we are much more than just rational beings. We are certainly emotional beings, but we are much more than just emotional beings. We are certainly a composition of material, but we are much more than just material. The same can be said for all the other theorized conceptions of what man is. Essentially, without the light of the Word, without the power of the Word to open our eyes, which we understand involves the work of the Spirit of God, we cannot make sense of who we are, let alone the world, and the God behind the world.

**Our Response to the Word**

How then are we to respond to the Word? It was not

---

25. Runner, *The Relation of the Bible to Learning*, 72.

Blind men and the elephant, 1907 American illustration.

meant to be another book, simply shelved away for our casual reference and reading. It was meant to be the lens by which we can see the world, and the guiding principle by which we can order our lives. Well, let me tell you how we ought to respond to the Word: *We are to submit to its authority.* That is to say, we are to submit to its truth claims. And that implies renouncing our pretended self-sufficiency, our own presuppositions, in order to embrace the presuppositions of Scripture and depend upon the One whom the Word reveals.

If it is a proper understanding we desire, we first require a proper understanding of ourselves. And if we hope to have a proper understanding of ourselves, we need *ultimately* a proper understanding of God. Our understanding of God, man, and creation are intimately tied together. We see this by virtue of the fact that man was created in the image of God as revealed by the Word. And without the Word, we cannot know such things. As I had said earlier, our sin already hampers our efforts to know the truth independently, but we are also finite beings that can only attain *true* knowledge when it is in relation to the Sovereign Creator God. Without Him, man is essentially left to grasp about in the dark. I mean, if such a God were to be somehow erased by a magic eraser, borrowing from Friedrich Nietzsche's thought, we would lose the meaning behind everything. This is what Van Til argued. We are left asking "What does it mean to be man?" "What does it mean to be moral?" "What does it mean to be alive?" In man's radical autonomy, in his quest to do away with God in every respect, man actually digs himself his own hole. He is at a loss, a *devastating* loss, not only philosophically, but *totally*. Man can find no true answers to his questions, not independently from the divine THESIS. It is the WORD that reveals to us the God behind creation, and in light of that, that reveals our own selfhood, "in its radical, integral unity."[26]

Why yield to the Word? Because apart from having the *thinkware* by which we can understand the world and order our lives, we are also promised life. And life

---

26. Ibid., 35.

not in the abstract sense, but in the person of Jesus, and how that is applied to us by the Spirit of God. The ordering of our lives would be nothing more than mere moralism without the redeeming life that Christ brings. And it is one of the many blessings of surrendering to the Word. And I do not mean surrendering solely in a *spiritual* sense, but in a *total* sense. The Word does not reveal to us a privatized, devotional piety, it reveals to us a faith that relates to every aspect and sphere of life. It is quite literally a *world-and-life* view. And blessed are those who submit to it, blessed are those who read it, who study it, who meditate upon it, and who apply its truths. Here are a few passages that speak towards that blessedness:

From the historical writings, the book of Joshua, chapter 1, verse 8:

> "This Book of the Law shall not depart from your mouth, but you shall meditate on it day and night, so that you may be careful to do according to all that is written in it. *For then you will make your way prosperous, and then you will have good success.*"

From the book of Psalms, chapter 1, verses 1-3:

> "Blessed is the man who walks not in the counsel of the wicked, but his delight is in the law of the Lord, and on his law he meditates day and night. *He is like a tree planted by streams of water that yields its fruit in its season, and its leaf does not wither. In all that he does, he prospers.*"

From the mouth of Jesus, in the *Gospel according to Matthew*, chapter 7, verses 24-26:

> "Everyone then who hears these words of mine and does them will be *like a wise man who built his house on the rock*. And the rain fell, and the floods came, and the winds blew and beat on that house, *but it did not fall, because it had been founded on the rock*. And everyone who hears these words of mine and does not do them will be like a foolish man who built his house on the sand."

And from the pen of James, in the first chapter of his letter, verse 25:

> "But the one who looks into the perfect law, the law of liberty, and perseveres, being no hearer who forgets but a doer who acts, *he will be blessed in his doing*."

As I look to bring our first session to a close, the corpus of the divine THESIS, the message and the understanding provided by the *inscripturated* revelation of God, is not to be treated lightly or to be laid to rest on deaf ears; they are *weighty*, weighty words of life. And given that it was always meant to be the very guiding and directing principle of our lives, since the moment it was first progressively revealed, it should be of no surprise to us that the Bible has endured to this day in spite of great tribulations. When the Babylonians, for example, destroyed Jerusalem in c. 586/587 BC, they destroyed everything, the walls, the temple, the beautiful artwork—and whatever was *not* destroyed was looted. And yet, in spite of this, the ancient texts endured.[27] When the Romans destroyed Jerusalem in AD 70, they too destroyed the temple. This was where the Torah and the books of prophecy were stored, and they too would have fallen victim to the flames. And yet, these texts have endured.[28] Of course, the New Testament texts were no stranger to these conditions. Before the sanction of the Christian religion by the Emperor Constantine, the biblical texts were outlawed and deemed a threat to Roman religion, governance, and life. Texts were confiscated and burned; their discovery reported to Roman authorities, and their owners arrested and punished.[29] This was most vigorous under the Emperors Galerius and Diocletian, between the years AD 303 to 311—a time in which Christians were burned alive and fed to animals in the colosseum.[30] And yet, in spite of all this persecution, in spite of every attempt to censor the biblical text, to expunge it from existence, and to intimidate those who clung to it, it has rigorously endured. I can go on further in relation to its miraculous history, but our next speaker will have much to say about that. The point is, it has endured to such an extent that it sets itself well apart from any other book, and it has done so simply because it is the *in-*

---

27. Steve and Jackie Green, *This Dangerous Book*, 202.

28. Ibid.

29. Ibid., 203.

30. Randall Price, *Searching for the Original Bible* (Eugene, OR.: Harvest House, 2007), 52, 157.

*spired* Word of God.

Being, therefore, the *inspired* Word of God, it calls us to respond to its revelation. To submit to its truth, and to embrace it as the divine THESIS that it is for our understanding and ordering of all of life. To not heed its call, to not surrender to the One who IS the Word, Jesus Christ—the One in whom the diverse Scriptures find their unity,[31] the One who gave His life in order that we might be redeemed from our sinful state—is not only to remain in the lie, in the ANTITHESIS, lost in the dysphoria it produces, it also ensures our condemnation, and the judgment that awaits us for our unforgiven sin. To renounce our own presuppositions and to embrace that of Scripture is, in truth, the acquirement of wisdom: *to see things for what they truly are; to see our human context within the framework of the whole of created reality. It is the divine principle by which to direct our goings.*

---

31. Runner, *The Relation of the Bible to Learning*, 24.

# IV

# THE REFORMATION
# & THE SPANISH

**Date:**   January 13, 2024
**Context:** The Theological Seminars
**Setting:** Sevilla Chapel, St. Catharines,
    Ontario, Canada

## Introductory Remarks

IT IS WITH immense gratefulness that I stand before you
here today at Sevilla Chapel. As many of you know, the
Cántaro Institute was founded alongside Sevilla, and it
has always been our intention that there might be some
symbiotic relationship between the two. On the one
hand, Sevilla has provided ample opportunity for the
development and delivery of reformed doctrinal teaching and worldview training, and Cántaro has been able
to package that content in such a way that it can be

disseminated through the Institute's respective distribution channels. And while the Institute does not rely solely on the Chapel—nor does the Chapel rely upon the Institute—both entities have benefited immensely from each other. I think back to two years ago, for example, when one of the Institute's board members, Rev. Daniel J. Lobo, came to visit us from Costa Rica in order to lecture on the reformed doctrines of grace. I remember also, just last year, that one of the Institute's associates, Nathan Diaz, came from Mexico to speak on how to read and interpret the book of Revelation, which was a challenge to those amongst us who still have not cut ties with dispensationalism. Both those teachings made their way to our online resource offerings and they have continued to benefit the church at large. In truth, the relationship between the Institute and the Chapel has been fruitful, more so than we first realized, and for that I am grateful to God.

Well, it is in light of that context that I stand here this morning to inaugurate a collaborative project between the Cántaro Institute and Sevilla Chapel, "The Theological Seminars". This collaborative project constitutes of bi-monthly seminars, or lectures, each on a different subject matter, with the objective of providing what is generally conceived as seminary-level education but presented and delivered in a condensed but intensive form. It may not compare to a full-year seminary course, but for those who do not have the time nor the funds, this may be a fruitful introduction to the high-level theological training available at most re-formed academic institutions, and which will no doubt prepare you, one way or another, for future studies. It has always been the intention of the Institute to take what is generally lofty and complex in the world of Christian academia, most particularly what is *biblical*, given all the bloated fluff that has been liberalizing our higher educational institutions, and make it accessible for the layperson. And the launch of "The Theological Seminars" is one way we are hoping to achieve that.

This morning we then launch the first of these seminars, or lectures, with a focus on church history, most specifically, the Spanish Reformation. As most of you will have realized by now, we have provided each of you with a textbook, not because today's subject is based on that book, but rather because the book pro-vides the necessary and complementary context from which we can frame and understand much of what we will examine today. The book, titled *The Unquenchable Flame: Discovering the Heart of the Reformation* by Mi-chael Reeves, is one of my favourite publications which I have long been recommending to first-time students of the reformation. You will also find before you a pen, a notebook, and a few refreshments and snacks to keep you hydrated, fed, and attentive. And if at some point during the course of the lecture you have a question, you are free to ask during our scheduled breaks, of which we will have two given that we have a total of three hours together.

## The Motive Behind the Study

Now, before we enter into the bone and marrow, so to speak, of the subject matter, there is the simple question of "Why begin with this subject?" And, "Why study this subject in particular?"

The reason why we are beginning with *this* subject, and not another, has a lot to do with both the Cántaro Institute and Sevilla Chapel. Both draw their names from different elements of the sixteenth-century Spanish reformation, and both these names communicate a story. You will eventually come to see what that is when we get to those respective elements. As for the second question, which could be rephrased as "Why do I need to study this subject?" Let me answer with the following:

For nearly all confessional Christians, that is to say, believers who hold to a reformed confession, whether that be the Heidelberg Catechism, the Canons of Dordt, the Westminster Confession, the 1689 Baptist Confession, etc., there is a general awareness of where their convictions came from *historically*. They can trace back their beliefs to the reformed communities that came about as a result of the protestant reformation. They have, in other words, a very rich reformational heritage. The French, for example, can think back to the Huguenots, those French protestants who persisted even after violent persecution, some even settling in Canada during the colonial years. Samuel de Champlain (1604-1616), one of the colonial leaders for New

"Martin Luther and his family" by G. A. Spangenberg (1866).

France (present-day Quebec) of the seventeenth century, was generally friendly and tolerable towards the Huguenots. The French and Swiss also have a reformational giant to refer to, John Calvin (1509-1564), who is often credited as the greatest reformed theologian of the whole reformation movement. In fact, today we have the *Institutes of the Christian Religion* available in multiple languages, which proved to be his magnum opus. The British have William Perkins (1558-1602), who wrote *The Reformed Catholic*, amongst other works. They also have William Tyndale (c. 1494-1536), one of the translators of the English Bible, who was influenced by Luther, and several more that are presently outside of our scope of study. Speaking of Luther, the Germans and Lutherans of all ethnicities today have Martin Luther (1483-1546), the catalyst of the reformation movement and author of *On the Bondage of the Will*, amongst several other works. Just by referring to these names, and some of the works they have produced, I am but merely scratching the surface of reformation history, because in truth there are still others to mention, such as Jan Hus, Ulrich Zwingli, Pierre Viret, etc. To put it simply, the reformation spread across Europe. And yet, if you were to ask a confessional Spanish believer what they know concerning their *Hispanic* protestant heritage, they would know very little. And I think the same can be said of any person today who comes from a land, a nation, or a culture where protestant beliefs were punished so severely and so persistently. That is one of the reasons why no one has heard, or speaks of the Spanish reformation, because the imposed belief by Spanish historians is that there was none. And if what they mean is the establishment of the reformation in Spain and its impact on its cultural development and thought, then we could all agree, but they go further than that as to dismiss it as nothing of importance. The Spanish reformation did happen, it just did not have an effect on Spain, not in a positive way that is. It is impossible to expect a reformation to have a positive national or cultural impact when the people refuse such a reformation. And the Catholic authorities of the sixteenth-century made it sure that the people were against the idea of a reformation. It was to be against it, or be tried by the Inquisition, tortured, and eventually burned at the stake. And yet, in spite of this, the Spanish reformation proceeded with those faithful protestants who were, in the end, exiled abroad; it could be said that it proceeded well away from its *madre patria* (motherland), and sowed seeds that are now giving fruit today, most particularly in Latin America, in ways they have not done so before.

This is why we must study this forgotten subject, because what God had started in that sixteenth-century amongst the Spanish people was not extinguished, and though it was interrupted in a certain sense by the machinations of man, it is rising up now without its past historic opposition. So, if we want to understand what God is doing now, in the midst of His Spanish-speaking church, not just here but in Latin America and wherever the Spanish-tongue is spoken, then we need to understand how it first began. And that which began so many years ago, in the sixteenth-century, was a spiritual awakening that was the result of the rediscovery of the biblical gospel message, and to amplify what that meant, we might put it this way: *it was a rediscovery of what the written revelation of God has to say about every aspect of life.*

### The Protestant Reformation

We begin with what many historians have referred to as the catalyst of the reformation. In the sixteenth-century, all across Europe, the Catholic Church had ramped up the sale of indulgences. For those unfamiliar with "indulgences", they were pieces of paper provided by the church that supposedly reduced a person's time in purgatory and sped their way to heaven in comparison to not having one. The notion of indulgences already appears unbiblical to us at first mention for a number of reasons, including the unbiblical idea of purgatory, which is nowhere found in the Scriptures, as well as the idea that we can pay our way into heaven, which is also absent in Scripture, and in some cases—such as when Simon the Magus attempted to buy the Holy Spirit's power from the apostle Peter (Acts 8:9-25)—is strongly and explicitly condemned. What use does God have of money? Is He not the owner of all the earth? Are not all the gems of the universe His own? Can a man make Him any richer? Or any poorer? In truth, man owns nothing directly, because everything is the Lord's, and whatever man has is whatever God has willed for him to have. God gives, and He takes away. Think of Job in the Old Testament. Well, the sale of indulgences can be traced back as early as the eleventh and twelfth century, which was when purgatory began to be taught more amply. And in those times, the sale of indulgences were in a different form. Unlike what we see in Luther's time, in the eleventh and twelfth centuries, as the Catholic church sought to reclaim Christian lands from Muslim invaders, what would be called "*La Reconquista*", the popes offered "full remission of sins" in exchange for a person's participation in the wars.[1]

---

1. L. G. Duggan, "indulgence", *Encyclopedia Britannica*.

"Peter's conflict with Simon Magus" by Avanzino Nucci (1620).

This was considered the first "indulgences", and it originated from papal decree. Of course, because this was not a biblical idea, the people needed some convincing, and this led to medieval theologians in the twelfth and thirteenth centuries to develop a theory of penance. To not stray from the subject at hand, it can simply be said that indulgences could only be administered by popes

Accessed December 14, 2023, https://www.britannica.com/topic/indulgence.

or in some cases archbishops and bishops in order to assist people with the management of their sin debt. And as you could imagine, in the same way that there are various financial aid packages in our society today, within the Catholic church, there were different kinds of indulgences, some that paid off your sin debt in full (which was called "plenary indulgences") and some that paid off your sin debt in part (which was called "partial indulgences").[2] The sale and provision of indulgences has a long and complex history, but I believe we have enough context to understand the catalyst of the reformation.

In the sixteenth century, particularly within the region where Martin Luther resided, there was a Dominican friar who went about from town-to-town preaching about the hellfire that awaited all sinners and the mercy that the Catholic church offered through the sale of indulgences. Purchase an indulgence, and your sins were forgiven, assured by the pope who was Christ's vicar on earth. Well, the way this Dominican friar went about his work—his name was Johann Teztel (c. 1465-1519) by the way—irritated Luther, who by this time was not only a monk, but a learned doctor at the Wittenberg monastery. It should be noted that prior to his contention with Tetzel and the sale of indulgences, Luther had already caused a bit of a stir by earlier questioning the Church's scholastic theology. On September 4, 1517, he had written his *Disputation Against Scholastic The-*

---

2. Ibid.

*ology* which was about 97 theses.[3] Perhaps this piqued the interest of the inhabitants of Wittenberg, because shortly after this, on October 31, 1517, Luther would go on to nail on the chapel door his famous 95 Theses, or his *Disputation on the Power and Efficacy of Indulgences.* And while this was in Latin, and written in academic language, and was meant to stir an academic debate on indulgences at the university in Wittenberg, his 95 Theses were taken from the chapel door, reproduced at the printing press, and distributed to all the people. This really caused a stir, and the people were very much in support of Luther because he had called out Rome's unbiblical affairs and was calling, at least in the eyes of the people before it was explicitly stated by Luther, for a church-wide reformation.[4] Luther was not clueless, of course, as all of this unfolded, he knew that the pope had ramped up the sale of indulgences because he needed money for the construction of the basilica of St. Peter, but as he states in Thesis 86:

> Why does not the pope, whose wealth today is greater than the wealth of the richest Crassus, build the basilica of St. Peter with his own money rather than with the money of poor believers?

---

3.  H. J. Hillerbrand, "Martin Luther", *Encyclopedia Britannica.* Accessed January 2, 2024, https://www.britannica.com/biography/Martin-Luther.

4.  See Carl E. Koppenhaver and Martin Luther, *Martin Luther & the 95 Theses* (Jordan Station, ON.: Cántaro Publications, 2024).

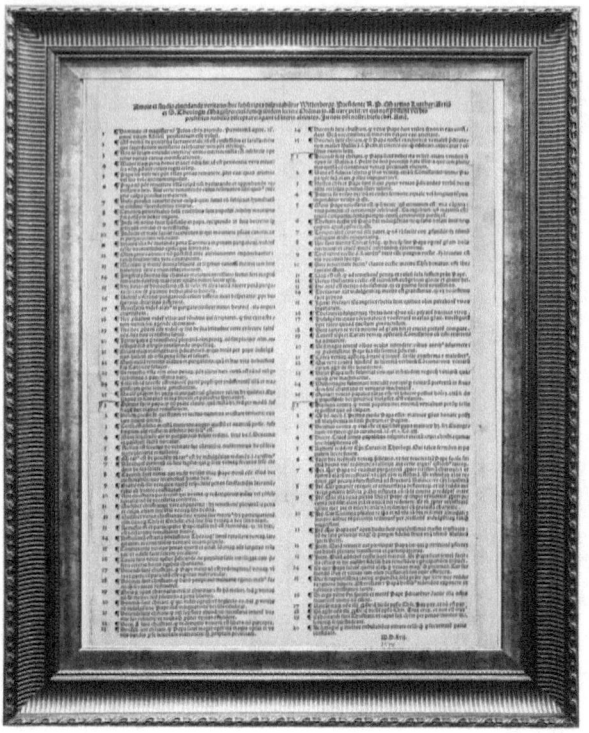

A single page printing of Ninety-five Theses in two columns.

Our focus of attention is not Luther today, but he is vital to what would later happen in Spain. What needs to at least be said is that, because of this event, because of Luther's 95 Theses, Luther had unknowingly sparked a flame that would spread across Europe and cause much turmoil and division in what were originally solely Catholic lands. We might see things from the eyes of men, but when we choose to see things from the eyes of God, which is to be informed by God's inscripturated revelation, we can see God dismantling the godless and corrupt machinations of men and rescuing His people from the lie and restoring them in the truth.

One might wonder why the people were so lost and ignorant under the teachings of the Catholic church, but the answer is found in the fact that the Bible was not available in the common vernacular tongue. Very few read Greek, few read Hebrew, and few read Latin, so even if they were to have held a Bible in their hands, it would have been useless to them. This meant that they had to depend on what the studied men of Rome had to say. And as it concerned interpretation, none could question what the pope interpreted; his word was to be treated as equal in authority to the Christ. This allowed such pagan ideas such purgatory and indulgences to proliferate the church at large, and that goes on to explain the significance of Luther's work, because after the 95 Theses, in 1518, Luther had reached a new understanding of salvation, not by inventing it, nor by meditating upon Roman Catholic thought, but by discovering it as he read and studied the Scriptures without the skewed dogma of Rome. One only needs to read the life of Martin Luther and the works he produced to understand how significant a schism had been wrought between Catholic Rome and the growing protestant movement. You also have to understand that it was not Luther's intent to split from Rome, he had not envisioned a splitting of the church in Europe, but rather, a reformation of the Catholic institution.

But with the unwavering stubbornness and hardness of heart of the pope and his subjects, a split became inevitable, and no matter how hard Rome would try, the fire had spread and it would not die down. The more one attempts to quash the truth, the more it disseminates, and the more one persecutes the faithful, the more the true faith spreads. God had called His elect out from the corrupt institution and towards reformation, in order that the gospel of God's grace might be recovered, and the whole counsel of God liberated from the ivory pillars of Catholic scholastic scholarship. As the English translator and reformer, William Tyndale, desperately desired, that a humble ploughboy could read and recite Scripture in his own tongue. The very thought of a humble ploughboy knowing God and knowing Him intimately through the written Word was unthinkable to Catholic Rome, it would be the undoing of its power and manipulation, but it was the very heart of the protestant reformation. No glory to the pope, all glory to the God who saves.

**Early Protestant Centers in Spain**

Moving now from Wittenberg to Spain, and not just in geography but in the passing of time as well, eventually the reformed ideas of Luther—and also John Calvin, who also had emerged on the scene as part of the protestant movement—reached Spanish lands. How did they reach Spanish lands? We can only assume, based on the historical records we have available to us today, that they were smuggled in by various means and at various ports. One particular smuggler that I believed would be worth bringing to our attention was Julián (Julianillo) Hernandez (xvi-1560). He also went by the name *Julian le Petit* in French.

### *Julián (Julianillo) Hernandez*

Julian was a Spaniard born in Valladolid, which would become one of two protestant centers in Spain, the other being Seville. While we do not have enough historical data to determine when he was born, we do know that he did not remain in Spain. He was partly raised in Germany, according to the testimony of Padre Martin de Roa (1560-1637), where he worked in the booming print industry. It seems almost providential, *perhaps it was providential,* that the reformation took place around the same time as the invention of the printing press (1436). Well, Julian would go on to be a skilled typesetter, which primarily concerned the interior design of books and pamphlets, and this allowed him to visit various parts of Europe. And given the close relation of the reformation movement and the printing press, it should not be a surprise that Julian was exposed to extensive reformational ideas from Germany and the Netherlands. This exposure would only grow as he became a proofreader and a stenographer. Well, at some point prior to the year 1550, Julian became a protestant, and between the years 1550 and 1559, he dedicated his time to smuggling into Spain

View of the city of Seville, (Spain), from the Triana neighborhood. The Fleet of the Indies, a fleet of galleons that connected the city with the American viceroyalties, arrived via the Guadalquivir River, by Alonso Sánchez Coello (c. 1531 – 8 August 1588).

various protestant works, most notably the Spanish New Testament translations by Juan Perez de Pineda, which was a precursor to Casiodoro de Reina's full Spanish Bible translation. I think it can be well said that without Julian's efforts to smuggle reformational material into Spain, the protestant centers of Valladolid and Seville would have suffered. The recovery of the biblical gospel, of God's truth, could only be possible with the inscripturated revelation of God in the vernacular tongue.

Tragically, Julian was eventually found out by the Spanish Inquisition, most likely betrayed, and after his arrest and his trial before the *Tribunal del Santo Oficio de la Inquisicion*, which was located in Seville, he was condemned, tortured in the most barbarous methods, and after having several of his bones dislocated, brought out to be burned at the stake in public for all to see. The date of his martyrdom is recorded as December 22, 1560. But Julian did not meet death with a whimper, nor did he quietly depart to the Lord's presence. It is said that while he was being carried to the stake, in such excruciating pain, he sang aloud a carol that annoyed his persecutors. It was "The friars go vanquished, they go vanquished! The wolves go running, running they go" (¡Vencidos van los frailes, vencidos van! Corridos van los lobos, corridos van). What did he mean by this? I am sure we can speculate many things, but what I believe is most apparent is that the decision to burn him at the stake, as with many other protestants, was an admission of defeat. The Inquisition had doubtlessly tried various times to convert protestants back to the Catholic faith, and there were certainly several who recanted as a result of their shallow faith, but Julian was not one of them. And the failure of these Inquisitorial agents, and the friars who worked along with them to convince these men of their heresy, was due to the fact that these men (and women as well) knew the Scriptures well enough to affirm and defend the truth. And so, the friars had no choice but to admit defeat before the truth, and the wolves had no choice but to quit their assault, handing these men and women over to death. Why? Because the gospel was too bright to put out with the lie, and the faith that it birthed was too dangerous for what the devil had wrought in such a corrupt Catholic institution. Better to put to death than to leave alive. The transformation of Spain could not be left as a potential, no matter how unlikely, it had to be completely snuffed out.

I do not want to get too ahead of myself. There will be time to explain the *auto-da-fé* that took place in Seville, but still a word of how the reformation infiltrated Spanish lands. Perhaps the most informative historical document that we have for how this may have taken place is the *Artes de la Inquisicion Espanola* published in 1567. The work was written by a supposed Raimundo Gonzalez de Montes, and I say "supposed" because we do not have a historical record of this person. What is most likely, and this has continued to be debated amongst scholars, is that this was a pseudonym used by either of two Spanish reformers who were once monks in Seville, those being Casiodoro de Reina and Antonio del Coro.[5] The consensus is inconclusive, with some leaning towards Reina and others towards Coro. In any case, it is a work that the Institute wants to bring back into print and to translate into English and modern Spanish for present-day readership. When that task is completed, hopefully within the next year or two, the work will then be much more widely accessible for research purposes. But to avoid getting side-tracked again, let me try to best frame our content, in light of what evidence has been made available to us today,

---

5.   B. A. Vermaseren, "Who Was Reginaldus Gonsalvius Montanus?", *Bibliothèque d'Humanisme et Renaissance*, Vol. 47, No. 1 (1985).

with a narrower focus on Seville, from which various Spanish reformers emerged.

## The Observantine Hieronymites

In the monastery of San Isidro del Campo, which laid a few miles northwest of Sevilla, there was a religious order that, arguably, if they had persisted, held the potential to deeply influence the culture and development of Spain. This order was known as the Observantine Hieronymites. I am not going to enter into the details of the order, especially considering that more research needs to be done on the matter, but what I can say is that the order gave expression to a distinctive Spanish spirituality. What do I mean by that? Well, historian Lewis J. Hutton writes that the Hieronymite Order could have well "achieved an industrial technology and a European type of capitalism", which was linked with its emphasis on "manual labor" as a "renascence of the initial program of the Franciscans... a characteristic of those who first followed the Hieronymite expression of the religious life."[6] To summarize this more succinctly, this could be understood as an early development, though still very raw in its form, to worshiping God in all aspects of life, and not solely perceived as within the confines of that which scholastic thought taught as "sacred" under the institutional church. It was the very beginning, the early embers, of what later we would see

6.  Lewis J. Hutton, "The Spanish Heretic: Cipriano de Valera", *Church History*, Cambridge University Press, Vol. 27, No. 1 (March, 1958), 23.

elsewhere in Europe as the "protestant work ethic."[7] A discussion for another time, especially as more research is conducted on the subject. You would be surprised how little research has been done on early protestant work in Spain, and I think it has a great deal to do with the pride of Spanish Catholicity which has supressed much of the interest and relevant evidences.

Well, as the reformation began to spread throughout Europe, reformed ideas reached the brothers of the monastery in the 1550s, and many of them in time would become protestants. They were not *outward* protestants because they knew the Inquisition was a growing danger and threat. But they harboured the desire to disseminate reformed ideas across Spain, and eventually the New World, in order to bring about a full-fledged reformation under the teaching of the Word of God. Several formed part of this group of protestant monks, though not all were converted, and some even were responsible for calling the Inquisition's attention to what was transpiring within the monastery, not for reasons having to do with orthodoxy and

---

7. "The pioneering sociologist Max Weber was the first to draw attention to the Protestant work ethic. In his book *The Protestant Ethic and the Spirit of Capitalism*, published in 1904, [he] studied the phenomenal economic growth, social mobility, and cultural change that accompanied the Reformation. He went so far as to credit the Reformation for the rise of capitalism" in Gene Edward Veith, "The Protestant Work Ethic", *Ligonier Ministries*. Accessed January 15, 2024, https://www.ligonier.org/learn/articles/protestant-work-ethic.

doctrine, but out of envy with the growing influence of protestant-leaning expositors and teachers.[8]

The first of these Spanish protestants of Seville that I wanted to call our attention to was Constantino Ponce de la Fuente (1502-1560), a name not commonly known but worth remembering as part of our protestant heritage, particularly for those who speak the Spanish tongue of Cervantes.

### Constantino Ponce de la Fuente

Ponce de la Fuente, or also known as Dr. Constantino, was born in San Clemente, in the province of Cuenca. He had received a theological education at the Universidad de Alcala and performed his ministerial work in Seville, arriving in 1533. Dr. Constantino is recorded as being the chief preacher of the cathedral. He was popular with the people of Seville, and as a result he was honoured for his writings. One of his most famous writings is *The Confession of a Sinner*, as well as the *Exposition of the First Psalm Divided In Six Sermons*, and several others which the Institute is currently working to put into print in modern English and Spanish, similar to the other work I had mentioned before. In fact, I think it can be well said that the Cántaro Institute has every intention of recovering historic Spanish protestant works that have been left to forgotten history. Well, returning to Dr. Constantino, his ministerial service in Seville happened to have been during the time when

---

8.  See Hutton, "The Spanish Heretic", 26-27.

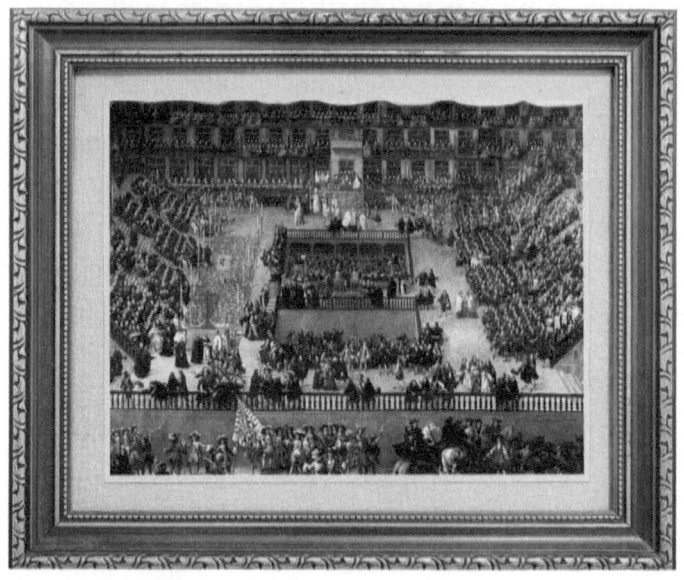

1683 painting by Francisco Rizi depicting the auto de fé held in
Plaza Mayor, Madrid, in 1680.

the city became a central point for the Spanish protestant reformation. Something was brewing right under
the Inquisition's nose, and the Inquisition had not yet
uncovered all that was going on. It was not unusual
for Catholic theologians to have protestant sympathies,
and it was not technically illegal, the Dutch theologian Desiderius Erasmus who was immensely popular
in Spain being one such example, but Dr. Constantino
was not a sympathizer, he was a covert protestant. He
may have preached in the cathedral under the guise of
Roman Catholicism, but his teachings were influenced
by the reformation and his writings were drenched in
reformed ideas. Nowhere publicly did he claim to be

protestant, and this was enough to make the Inquisition mad because they suspected him, and yet had no evidence to condemn him. His brief departure from Seville did not appear to help him, because from the year 1548 to 1553, Dr. Constantino served as the King's chaplain and earned high respect for the content and delivery of his sermons. And if anything, this made him a bigger target for the Inquisition given the growing influence and respect he had. Eventually, Dr. Constantino was found out. He had been arrested, interrogated, and throughout he affirmed his catholicity, until evidence was presented which led to his confession. A woman who had attended his sermons at the cathedral had several reformed writings by Dr. Constantino which were explicitly reformed, it was exactly what the Inquisition needed, and it so happened that these writings were hidden and the Inquisition found them by accident.[9] Upon this discovery, Dr. Constantino admitted his protestant convictions, affirmed the biblical gospel, refused to recant and insisted that he would not abandon what the Scriptures so clearly taught. Before he could be executed, the Lord took his spirit while he laid in his dungeon. The records say he had died of illness, but only the Lord knows. This, of course, did not prevent the Inquisition from later digging up his remains in order to burn them at one of their *autos-da-fé*. While it is a tragically sad story, the life of Dr. Constan-

---

9.   See Marcelino Menéndez y Pelayo, *Historia de los heterodoxos españoles*, Vol. V (Madrid, Lib. de Victoriano Suárez), 1928.

tino is worth remembering, because he was very much a spiritual giant in the land of the Spanish reformers.

## *Auto-da-fé*

Prior to proceeding any further, if you are wondering what is an *auto-da-fé*, let me explain: An *auto-da-fé*, which meant "act of faith", was the ritual of public penance carried out between the fifteenth to nineteenth centuries of condemned heretics and apostates, imposed by the Inquisition as a punishment and enforced by civil authorities.[10] While it was the Inquisition that condemned heretics, it was the civil government which performed the act of execution. And the most extreme form was death by burning, often in the most gruesome manner in order to strike fear in the general populace. Of course, given the extremism of the Inquisition, which operated as without a leash, burning living people was not enough, constructing effigies for people not present and burning them allowed them to carry out their murderous agenda, and even digging up and burning those who had died before their planned execution. Generally, an *auto-da-fé* consisted of a Catholic mass, prayer, a public procession of those found guilty, and a reading of their sentences. It was also a form of penitence for public viewers, because they were seen as engaging in a process of reconciliation and provided with the chance to confront their own sins and to be

---

10. See Toby Green, *Inquisition: The Reign of Fear* (New York, NY.: St. Martin's Press, 2007).

forgiven by the Church.

Having then explained the *auto-da-fé*, let me now bring two more individuals to our attention, former brothers at the monastery of San Isidro, and spiritual giants in their own right. These individuals are Casiodoro de Reina (c. 1520-1594) and Cipriano de Valera (1531-1602). If their names sound familiar, it is because of the present-day Reina-Valera Bible translations, but I will explain that shortly.

### Casiodoro de Reina

Reina is believed to have been born around the year 1520 in Montemolin in the province of Badajoz. He is recorded as always having had an interest in the Christian Scriptures and this led to him becoming a monk of the Hieronymite monastery in 1557. This means that he would have been acquainted with Dr. Constantino, perhaps even benefitted from his mentorship before his seizure. Reina's time as a monk, however, was not for very long. While at the monastery, he became a protestant, and this was likely the result of having read the smuggled reformed literature that was hidden there. According to some scholars, he is believed to have been a central figure in the growth and organization of the protestants in Seville during his short tenure.[11]

---

11. See Gordon A. Kinder, *Casiodoro de Reina: Spanish Reformer of the Sixteenth Century* (London, UK.: Tamesis Books Limited, 1975); Andrés Messmer, *Casiodoro de Reina: Su vida, Biblia y teología: Ensayos en honor del 500 aniversario de su nacimiento* (Madrid: Editorial CLIE, 2023).

When the protestant community was found out by the Inquisition, Reina was amongst the few that managed to escape. He first fled to Geneva, where he spent some time there, and departed in 1558 because he was unhappy with the doctrinal rigidity of John Calvin. He believed it was a "New Rome", but we would later find out that this was the case because Reina had friends who were actually heretics, such as Servetus who was a Unitarian, and such heretics were not welcome nor accepted in Geneva. There also appeared to be a general dislike of the Spanish on Calvin's part, probably because of the many heretics that came from Spanish lands, and this is later attested as to the reason why Valera, who was with Reina, departed as well. Well, after some time, Reina fled to England which had just opened its doors to protestant refugees under Queen Elizabeth. Not long before Elizabeth there was a terrible persecution of protestants under Queen Mary I (from 1553 to 1558), but things had changed with the coronation of Queen Elizabeth. England had become, under Elizabethan rule, a refuge for protestant foreigners. Reina, as well as Valera, after having sought consultation, accepted the invitation of refuge in England, and though both would go on to do different things and in different places, both would remain in contact with one another.

Having found refuge in London, England, in 1559, Reina petitioned and received the necessary permission from the Queen to plant a distinctly *Spanish* protestant church alongside the already existing French, Italian and Fleming consistories. He was granted the necessary permission from the English crown and partially succeeded in planting the Spanish congregation. I say "partially" because his work was not altogether completed with the church, he was later forced to flee as a result of meddling by the Inquisition's agents. To make a long story short, the Inquisition had supposed Spanish protestants in England who were contemplating a safe return to Spain, in exchange for their pardon they would have had to agree to do certain things for the Inquisition. They became covert agents, so to speak. No such pardon was afforded to those protestants within Spain, but it was considered a political victory if they managed to de-convert a protestant abroad and win them back to Catholic Spain. And even better if they inflicted harm upon the expatriated Spanish reformation. Well, after several attempts to defame and scandalize Reina, one attempt worked well enough to frighten Reina and to question his credibility, it had to do with sharing a bed with a younger man, and though both had committed no act of sin, the accusations were enough to force Reina and the young man to flee. It would later be revealed that the charges were false and made up by one who had ties to the Inquisition, but the ploy had accomplished its objective, which was to cause Reina to flee his protestant project in England.[12]

---

12. See Steven R. Martins, "Agents, Scandals and Gossip: Lessons from the Life of Reina", *Cántaro Institute*. Accessed January

However, Reina had managed, prior to his abrupt departure, to put together a reformed confession for the founding and recognition of his church, a confession which we can refer today as *The Spanish Confession of the Christian Faith* which the Institute, this past month, had finished translating into both English and modern Spanish and published for the first time in a bilingual format.

Most of you, if not all of you, should have received a copy of this Confession as Sevilla Chapel's year-end gift to you. Now, I know that reading historic confessions is not exactly a popular pastime, most within our circles tend to turn to them for research and study purposes. But while many of us are not accustomed to reading historic confessions, I believe it is worthwhile to read this confession by Reina, which, by the way, had been edited by his friend Valera. Why it is worthwhile you ask? Because of its historic significance, and because of how precious a treasure it is for our own protestant heritage. A treasure, not because it is the work of man, but rather because it is a work that was birthed as a result of God's grace through faith, as all reformed confessions are.

Let me now sum up the rest of Reina's contribution to the Spanish reformation. After fleeing England, Reina arrived in Frankfurt in 1564, by the way of Antwerp the year prior. There he settled with his family and

17, 2024, https://cantaroinstitute.org/agents-scandals-and-gossip-lessons-from-the-life-of-reina/.

wrote what I believe is his work *Artes de la Inquisición Española*. While there, Reina also completed what was his most major and time-consuming project, and perhaps the most significant accomplishment of the Spanish reformation movement, the complete translation of the Bible into Spanish. Reina's translation is no small feat, he had used a number of ancient texts that were available at his disposal to realize his translation, including the Ferrara Bible (Hebrew Bible) in Ladino, the Masoretic text, the Vetus Latina, the Receptus of Erasmus, and even various Syriac manuscripts. And he was not without assistance, Pérez de Pineda's earlier New Testament translation aided Reina in this full text edition. I will get to Pérez because he is worth mentioning briefly, but first a word about Valera.

### Cipriano de Valera

Reina's Bible translation was published in 1569, and was called *La Biblia del Oso* because of its front cover imagery, but we cannot speak of Reina's accomplishment without also mentioning Valera's later involvement. For those familiar with the history of the Spanish Bible, it would be Valera who would go on to revise and publish the second edition of the Bible in 1602, *La Biblia del Cántaro* (also call that because of its front cover imagery).[13] I will get to that, but first, a word on

---

13. See Steven R. Martins, "The Emblems of the Oso and Cántaro Bibles", *Cántaro Institute*. Access January 17, 2024, https://cantaroinstitute.org/the-emblems-of-the-oso-and-cantaro-bibles/.

Valera's emergence:

Cipriano de Valera (1531-1602) was born at Fregenal de la Sierra, Badajoz, north of Seville. He was a student for six years at the University of Seville, where he studied Dialectics and Philosophy and graduated with a bachelor's degree. It was in his early twenties that he became a member of the Order of Observantine Hieronymites, and there he served alongside Reina and several other protestants.[14] It is worth noting that Reina became very much a mentor for him, and this explains their close relationship in the future. Well, having come to accept the ideas of the reformation, he along with twenty other monks (at the least) would be declared protestant heretics by the Inquisition, but unlike many of the others, Valera managed to escape with Reina and found his place of refuge first in Geneva. While Reina did not particularly benefit from his time in Geneva, Valera did, becoming heavily influenced by Calvin's theology and translating into Spanish the great reformational treasure *The Institutes of the Christian Religion*, which articulates what we call today the "reformed doctrine" prior to the later development of the reformed confessions, including the Westminster Confession of Faith, Canons of Dordt, and the 1689 Baptist Confession of Faith, to name a few. One might argue whether these confessions would have come about

---

14. See Ivan E. Mesa, "'Open Your Eyes, O Spaniards': Cipriano de Valera – A Forgotten Spanish Protestant of the 16th Century", *The Banner of Truth* (Feb. 2015).

Portrait of Cipriano de Valera that appears in *La Biblia del Siglo de Oro.*

the way that they did without Calvin's contribution to the reformation. In truth, Calvin has proven to be by far the greatest theologian of the reformation era, and Valera would follow in his footsteps, eventually gaining the title "The Spanish Heretic" (*par excellence*) by the Inquisition because of his theological brilliance and excellence in polemical writing.

After his considerably fruitful time in Geneva, Valera would proceed to find refuge in England, as I had mentioned earlier, but instead of setting up home in London, Valera would go on to take a position at the University of Cambridge as Professor of Theology, eventually becoming a Fellow of Magdalene College. And in the year 1565, he received his Master of Arts from the University of Oxford, testifying of his intellectual prowess. From between this time to his move to London, we do not have much historical data, but what we can say is that Valera would go on to become a vital asset in England's religious war with Spain, writing several works and translating the works of other reformers to disseminate into Spanish lands as a form of artillery fire. His most notable works are *Los Dos Tratados del Papa y la Misa* and *Un Tratado para confirmar en la fe cristiana a los cautivos de Berberia*, both of which the Institute is planning to translate and republish, and Lord-willing, before the Spring, we will have the second of those two treatises in print for reading.

Well, not to stagnate there, Valera proceeded to follow up his academic career with a move to London to take over the pastoral position that Reina had left vacant. Some scholars believed the church dissolved immediately after Reina's departure, or at least shortly after Valera arrived as his replacement, but we have no reason to believe that this dissolution took place. Valera was very much involved in the development and presentation of the Spanish Confession, and we have every reason to believe that he felt very invested in what Reina, his mentor, had begun in London amongst the

Spanish protestant refugees. Now, besides this fact of Valera's move to London, we do not know much more about Valera, aside also from the fact that he married and had children. The last historical note we have on record of his life is the publication of *La Biblia del Cántaro* in 1602, after of which we find no more mention of his name. But what a significant contribution he made to the expatriated Spanish reformation. *La Biblia del Cántaro* was a revision of Reina's prior work, where he did not touch much of Reina's actual translation work, in any major way at least, but did re-organize the content of the Bible's content to better reflect the organization of other translated protestant Bibles. This includes the omission of the apocrypha, and the grouping of Old and New Testament books according to the order of which we have today in our own Bibles. No more needs to be said of the fact that these two translations, by Reina and Valera, became the literary foundation for the Reina-Valera Bible translations for today. And for this reason, ample tribute is paid to these Spanish reformers by present-day Hispanic Bible societies.

### Juan Pérez de Pineda

I had said that I was going to say a word about Juan Pérez de Pineda (c. 1500-1567), and I should, given that we see his work prior to that of Reina and Valera, so he is also worthy, in my estimation, of our consideration. Pérez is believed to have been born in Montilla, Cordoba. For a time, he served as an overseer of finances for the Emperor Charles V (1500-1558). And being a man of sharp mind, Pérez diligently occupied the role of Rector for the Colegio de la Doctrina (College of Doctrine) in Seville, a term of office that would witness the city becoming the principal breeding ground for Protestantism in Spain. We are not told, whether by historical evidence or current scholarship, when *exactly* Pérez converted to Protestantism, but it would have been prior to the arrest of Juan Gil in 1551 by the Spanish Inquisition. As the records testify, Pérez managed to escape the religious persecution that arose, and thanks to his escape, he managed to contribute significantly towards the Spanish reformation. In what ways? Well, in 1556, before Reina had printed his Spanish translation of the whole Bible, *La Biblia del Oso* (1569), Pérez printed his Spanish translation of the New Testament in Geneva, assisted by the earlier translation works of Francisco de Enzinas and Juan de Valdés.[15] His copies of the *Nuevo Testamento* were smuggled into Spain through various means, but most successfully by Julián Hernández (or Juliánillo) whom I had earlier mentioned. Pérez is also credited with writing the *Epístola Consolatoria* in 1560, which was written for the comfort and encouragement of the persecuted

---

15. Rafael Serrano, "El Nuevo Testamento publicado por Juan Pérez de Pineda", *Medium*. Accessed Jan. 4, 2024, https://medium.com/historia-de-la-biblia-en-espanol/el-nuevo-testamento-publicado-por-juan-perez-de-pineda-fe0bc608df5c

brothers and sisters in the faith.[16] This is a particular work which the Institute has acquired and which we hope to make available in both modern English and Spanish. But without getting distracted by an otherwise rewarding venture—towards the end of his life, Pérez would go on to serve as chaplain for the Duchess Renata de Ferrara (1510-1574) in France, who had made her territorial dominions a haven for protestants in need of refuge. On more than one occasion, she had provided refuge for those fleeing death for their faith, and she would be highly praised by the reformer John Calvin.[17] Returning again to Pérez, in his devoted pursuit of a full translation of the Bible into Spanish, one which would surpass the quality of his own efforts, he left upon his death in 1567 funds specifically designated for the project, funds which would later benefit Reina, who would make good use of Pérez's New Testament translation work for his *Biblia del Oso.*

Looking back now, so much more needs to be said about the Spanish reformation, and there are sever-

---

16. See "Obras digitalizadas de Juan Pérez de Pineda", *Biblioteca Digital Hispanica de la Biblioteca Nacional de España.* Accessed Jan. 1, 2024, http://bdh.bne. es/bnesearch/Search.do?numfields=1&field1=autor&-field1val=%22P%C3%A9rez%2c+Juan%22&field1Op=AND&exact=on&advanced=true&language=esEn/.

17. Ruth A. Tucker, "John Calvin and the Princess", *Christianity Today.* Accessed January 3, 2024, https://www.christianitytoday.com/history/2009/september/john-calvin-and-princess.html.

REFORMATION & CULTURE: SELECT LECTURES

al reformers that I have not yet had time to mention but which deserve just as much attention. In a short matter of time, however, I have managed to give you a condensed summary of what Spanish Catholics have refused to call "the Spanish reformation." There *was* a reformation, although it had been exiled from Spanish lands, and though it accomplished little when compared to those lands where the reformation was eventually embraced, it nonetheless happened. A small fire is still a fire when compared to a forest fire; in the same way, we cannot deny that there was such a thing as a "Spanish reformation." Of course, I cannot just leave the matter there. A suitable word does need to be said in order to close our subject properly, and that last word concerns what, if anything, reached the New World as a result of the Spanish reformation, and whether that humble reformation movement had any positive effect on the development of Spanish society.

**What Reached the New World?**

First, concerning what reformational material from the sixteenth century reached the Spanish-speaking New World. I explore this in greater length in the 2021 edition of the Institute's *La Fuente*, our Iberoamerican Journal for Christian Worldview—which, for those interested, will find available to download online for free—but to summarize what I had written: up until this date, there remains very few surviving extant documents of what reformational materials reached the

*La Biblia del Cántaro* is part of the extensive library of the linguist Rufino Cuervo, which is now preserved by the National Library of Colombia.

New World. What can be said, however, and this with a relatively high level of certainty, is that the works of Dr. Constantino Ponce de la Fuente, those being the *Exposición del Primer Salmo, Confesión de un Pecador, Sermón de Nuestro Redentor en el Monte,* and *Suma de Doctrina Cristiana,* were imported and distributed throughout the Spanish and Portuguese colonies, where, for example, the Franciscan bishop Juan de Zumarraga (first bishop of Mexico) applied his teachings to the Mesoamerican mission field.[18] There is evidence, in fact, that the Nahua and Zacatecas of Mexico were

---

18. Andrew L. Wilson, "The Unfortunate Fate of Luther in the Ibero-American World" in *Studies in Luther* (USA: Lutheran Forum, Summer 2009), 32.

instructed by Ponce's writings in the biblical basics of the Christian faith.[19]

What can also be ascertained is the introduction of the first full Spanish translation of the Bible, the *Biblia del Oso*, which was smuggled into Latin America shortly after its publication in 1569. Reina's edition, followed by Valera's later revision, the *Biblia del Cántaro*, were smuggled into the New World with several covert protestant communities willing to run the risk to receive them. And, thinking about it now, they would have been an invaluable treasure to those early protestant communities. Of course, in order to avoid detection, the Bibles had different images on their covers, and one such copy rests in the National Library Collection of Colombia, with a Pegasus image on the front. Scholarship associated with the Colombian Ministry of Culture claim that the copy corresponds to Valera's *Biblia del Cántaro*, and how it ended up in Colombia is unclear—only that it was found in the literary collection of the Colombian linguist Rufino José Cuervo Urisarri (1844-1911).[20] Unfortunately, given the Inquisition's presence in Ibero-America, the *Biblia del Oso* and all

---

19. Ibid.

20. Pablo Rodriguez J., "La Biblia del Oso," Biblioteca Nacional de Colombia. Accessed November 09, 2018, http://bibliotecanacional.gov.co/ es-co/colecciones/ biblioteca-digital/publicacion?nombre=La%20 Biblia%20del%20Oso&fbclid=IwAR25Mq14IT 6lhaA0ykv7i_3Fji582npAe-Ncdstu7zEI1d6jaqlzuppfj8/.

its later revised variants were soon after discovered and destroyed.[21] Very little made its way to the New World, and very little remains preserved today.

## Did the Spanish Reformation Impact the Hispanosphere?

And this brings me to the next matter, whether the Spanish reformation had a positive impact on the Hispanosphere. Unlike what can be said about the influence and development of the reformation on the Anglosphere, the reality of the Hispanosphere is quite stark. As a result of the Inquisition's efforts and the counter-reformation in Spain and the New World, the protestant reformation had little to no influence on the development of Hispanic religion and society. On the contrary, its absence gave way to animism, religious syncretism, and later modernism. As pastor and scholar Miguel Núñez writes in his book, *El Poder de la Palabra para Transformar una Nación*:

> The Latin American worldview has been mostly animistic, syncretistic and modernist… Animism has not only influenced the traditional Church of Rome, but also many of the anti-biblical beliefs manifested in "evangelical" churches that abuse the practice of the supernatural gifts of the Spirit. "Modernism" is the best way of labelling the worldview of the continent, mixed with

---

21. Cornelius Hegeman, *La Reforma en America Latina y el Caribe* (Guadalupe, Costa Rica: Editorial CLIR, 2017), 37-38.

Roman Catholicism, Deism and Animism.[22]

The absence of the reformational faith explains why Christian life in the Hispanosphere did not experience the same transformation and flourishing as that of Europe and North America, and why it failed to serve as an instrument for the transformation of its culture. In the end, culture can only possibly reflect the religious worldview of the people, culture is *the people's religion externalized*. It should be of no wonder then that Iberoamerican culture failed to exhibit the fruits of biblical, protestant convictions in its history, this is because there were none, and if there were, it was certainly anemic. That is not to discredit the present-day protestant churches that are working the mission fields, or the past missionaries who have long suffered to plant biblically reformed churches, it simply means that Protestantism, as a major cultural influencer (and transformative agent), has been absent for much of the Hispanosphere's history, but Lord-willing, not for long.

## How are we Contributing to the On-going Reformation?

How are we contributing to the on-going reformation? If by "we" I mean Christians everywhere in the Hispanosphere, then the response is simple, we are to adopt the same reformational spirit of the reformers,

---

22. Miguel Núñez, *El Poder de la Palabra para Transformar una Nación* (Medellín, Colombia: Poiema Publicaciones, 2016), 10.

which is expressed in the form of the Five Solas. We know these Five Solas as: *Sola Gratia, Sola Fide, Solus Christos, Sola Scriptura*, and *Soli Deo Gloria.* When articulated together, these Solas express that we are saved by grace alone, through faith alone, in Christ alone, according to Scripture alone, for the glory of God alone. If we were to elaborate on this, we can say that in respect to *Sola Gratia*, we would want to ensure that we never depart from the doctrine of God's grace, and not only in terms of our *understanding*, but in terms of our *practice*. In the same way, as it relates to *Sola Fide*, we would want to ensure that we never depart from the doctrine of justification through faith in Christ— and again, not only in terms of our *understanding* but also in terms of our *practice*. If we live in such a way that reflects that we are trying to earn God's favour, then we contradict the teachings of the Word and our confession. If we live in such a way that presupposes our self-righteousness, then we deny the truth of God's Word concerning our sinfulness and that righteousness can only be found in God, and that His righteousness can only be imputed to us in the Son, Jesus Christ. And similarly, as it relates to *Solus Christos*, we must always affirm that there is salvation in no one else but Jesus Christ alone. No mystic, no Hindu, no Buddhist, no Muslim, no one outside of Christ will find salvation in their own religion and false philosophies. Outside of Christ, we are dead in our sins, and liable to final and eternal judgment. And then we have *Sola Scriptu-*

*ra*, which is more than just adhering to it as our final authority for matters relating to doctrine and personal piety, but also as our final authority for all living and thinking. While it is true that the Bible is not a manual for every discipline and every activity done under the sun, it does provide us with the necessary parameters from which we can rightly understand things and determine how we ought to do things in obedience to God, our Creator. And then, last but not least, we have *Soli Deo Gloria*, that all that we believe, and all that we do, as guided by the Scriptures, is for the glory of God alone. In truth, as per the reformer John Calvin, God's creation and all that happens within it is the theater of God's glory.[23]

The Five Solas deserve to be examined as subjects altogether separate themselves, but in this condensed form I think we can understand how we can embody the reformational spirit. You see, that reformational phrase back then is still applicable to us now, it's the Latin phrase *Ecclesia semper reformanda*, and translated to our common tongue today, we understand it as "the church always reforming." *That* is the reformational spirit, not only in preserving what the reformation recovered as a result of its study of the Word, but seeking to always reform our thinking and living to the whole

---

23. See John Piper and David Mathis, "With Calvin in the Theater of God", *desiringGod*. Accessed Jan. 7, 2024, https://www.desiringgod.org/books/with-calvin-in-the-theater-of-god/.

counsel of the Word. And as we can see from then until now, the church has continued to mature, has continued to reform, and while we can certainly cite several setbacks and diversions, we cannot deny that we are at a much better place today in our theological development and Christian practice than times of old. And yet, we can also see what things we have forgotten, what things need to be taken up again—such as the study and implementation of the reformed confessions and catechisms—and what needs to be done that has not perhaps been done before. It is an almost endless cycle of self-reflection, meditation, and implementation, under the light of the Word; but it will come to full fruition when Christ returns. Until then, the Institute is doing its part to contribute toward the reformation and renewal of the church and culture. And Sevilla Chapel, well, as a small local church, we need to continue our study of the Word, explore its varied applications, and daily live it out. Without any embarrassment, and actually with much joy, we are, in our confession, a reformed community, distinctly Baptist, but reformed. And we join with other reformed communities, yes even our presbyterian brothers, in the distinctives of the Five Solas, and of the doctrines of grace, as affirmed by the historic reformed confessions. There is more to being reformed than this, we know, but for the sake of time, I must leave it at that.

And having said that, we have now come to the end of our study together. I leave with you the following parting words by the Spanish reformer Valera:

> Open your eyes... and forsaking those who deceive you, obey Christ and His Word which alone is firm and unchangeable for ever. Establish and found your faith on the true foundation of the Prophets and Apostles and sole Head of His Church.[24]

---

24. Cipriano de Valera, "A Todos los Fieles de la Nazion Española", in Juan Calvino, *Instituzion Relijiosa* (1536), traduzida al castellano por Cipriano de Valera en 1597. Vol. XIV of *Reformistas Antiguos Españoles* edited by Luis Usoz y Rio (Madrid, 1858), 12.; In place of "Hispanics", Valera uses the word "Spaniards", I substituted the word given our present context.

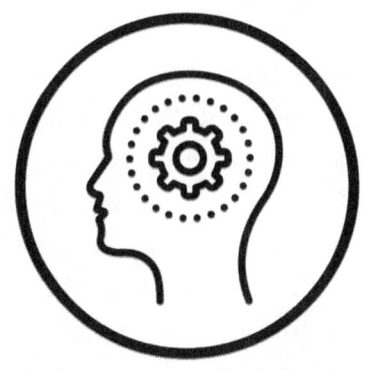

# V

# APOLOGETICS & RELIGIOUS WORLDVIEWS

**Date:**   March 9, 2024
**Context:** The Theological Seminars
**Setting:**  Sevilla Chapel, St. Catharines,
          Ontario, Canada

## Introductory Remarks

I WOULD LIKE to open this morning's seminar with the following quote by Cornelius Van Til, the 20th century Christian thinker who taught at Westminster Theological Seminary:

> I hold that belief in God is not merely as reasonable as other belief, or even a little or infinitely more probably true than other belief; I hold rather that unless you be-

lieve in God you can logically believe in nothing else.

Van Til was a reformed Presbyterian who is known for having developed a distinctly *Christian* apologetic, that is to say, a distinctly *biblical* discipline of defending the faith, or rather, of the *religious worldview* of Scripture. We are not going to look at apologetics as a broad discipline today—that will be for another day—but we are going to look at the concept of "worldview", which is an essential component to Christian apologetics. I might add, the concept of "worldview" extends well beyond the discipline of apologetics given its all-comprehensive nature. We could talk about philosophy, for example, and we would not be able to rid ourselves of the concept of worldview. The same can be said of any specialized discipline, or even matters of public thought and discussion. Worldviews, as we are about to see, are not only all-encompassing, but all-pervasive because of their very nature.

Much of what I have to share in today's seminar has been garnered through my readings of Van Til (1895–1987), his late students Greg L. Bahnsen (1948–1995), John M. Frame (1939–), Francis Schaeffer (1912–1984), and his contemporary Herman Dooyeweerd (1894–1977), who was based in the Netherlands. Towards the end of our time together, I will be sure to recommend several titles for your own reading, in addition to your assigned textbook, which, if you have yet to notice, is a title by H. Evan Runner, *The Relation of the Bible to Learning*, who was a student of both Van

Til and Dooyeweerd.

Faithful to the objective of these theological seminars, which is co-organized between Sevilla Chapel and the Cántaro Institute, I will be attempting to communicate what is often taught and expressed at the higher levels of education at a level that the common layperson can understand. And while we will be covering ample ground in a relatively short span of time, you will hopefully leave here with the most basic essentials concerning what is a worldview, how we can understand our world, and what we are to do.

## Why Study "Worldviews"?

If you are asking yourself why we need to understand the concept of a "worldview", the answer is linked to our pursuit of understanding reality for what it truly is. When you turn on the television, when you read the news, when you see what is taking place in our schools, legislatures, and the public square, the most common reaction is that of confusion. What exactly is going on? Where is Western culture going? Where did it come from? How do we make sense of all the moving parts and all the emerging ideas and concepts in what some people call a "progressive" society? It almost seems random, especially when one does not understand the underlying *worldviews* of our culture, but there are discernible patterns, there is some general order believe it or not, and it is simply a matter of understanding what is what, and the nature of that what. To put it more simply, if we hope to understand the world, if we hope to understand our present cultural moment, then we need to understand what a "worldview" is, especially considering the fact that every living person has a "worldview."

## What is a Worldview?

Let me first begin by defining what a worldview *is*. The term "worldview" is a translation from the German *Weltanschauung* and was first used by the philosopher Immanuel Kant (1724-1804). From within its context of German Idealism and Romanticism, it came to mean "a set of beliefs that underlie and shape all human thought and action." If I can put it more simply, I would simply say that a "worldview" can be defined as a "particular philosophy of life or conception of the world." It is essentially the *lens* through which we *see* and *interpret* the world. In my book, *Christian Apologetics*, I explain that a worldview consists of three essential components: (1) metaphysics; (2) epistemology; and (3) ethics. To put that in the vernacular, every worldview consists of beliefs concerning *reality* (metaphysics), *knowledge* (epistemology), and *morality* (ethics). In other words, what is what? How do we know that what? And how should we live in light of that? A worldview can therefore be understood *as a network of presuppositions, or preconceptions, through which we interpret the world.*

Immanuel Kant (1724-1804), Portrait, 1768.

Now, I tend to add the word "religious" right before the word "worldview", and the reason as to why I do this is to make clear that *all* worldviews are *religious* in nature. You can use the word "worldview" and it would still carry that same meaning, but because so many people misunderstand the *nature* of worldviews, I prefer to leave absolutely no doubt that every worldview is *religious* in nature. That means that the atheist, or the agnostic, has a worldview that is fundamentally *religious*, even if the tenets of his worldview deny the religious. What do I base this on? On Romans 1:18-23, which states:[1]

> [18] For the wrath of God is revealed from heaven against all ungodliness and unrighteousness of men, who by their unrighteousness suppress the truth. [19] For what can be known about God is plain to them, because God has shown it to them. [20] For his invisible attributes, namely, his eternal power and divine nature, have been clearly perceived, ever since the creation of the world, in the things that have been made. So they are without excuse. [21] For although they knew God, they did not honor him as God or give thanks to him, but they became futile in their thinking, and their foolish hearts were darkened. [22] Claiming to be wise, they became fools, [23] and exchanged the glory of the immortal God for images resembling mortal man and birds and animals and creeping things.

I am going to unpack what the apostle Paul wrote here under the inspiration of the Holy Spirit. In verse 18, we are told that the natural man, that is to say, the sinful and unregenerate man, knows the truth of God, as well as the truth of all things, but he *suppresses* the truth by his own sinful nature. Theologians have referred to this as the *noetic* effects of sin, the corrupting influence of our sinful nature on our intellectual (or cognitive) faculties. How does the natural man

---

1. *Editor's Note: Due to specific verse references in this chapter, verse reference numbers have been preserved wherever Scripture has been cited in this lecture transcript.*

know the truth to begin with? Verse 19 tells us that God has made the truth known to man by virtue of His creation. And that the truth of *who God is* can be discerned ever since the creation of the world, as we read in verse 20. But because of their sin, because of their suppression of the truth, verse 21 tells us that the sinful man exchanged the worship of the true God for the worship of creation. And thus, claiming to be wise (think of the brightest, most intellectual minds of our day who deny the truth of God) they prove to be fools, for they exchange the truth for the lie. There is therefore only *two* religious orientations, the *vertical*, and the *horizontal*. The *vertical* is the worship of God, and not just any "god", but the God who has revealed Himself through creation and through His inscripturated Word which serves as the only authoritative interpretation of creation. As a matter of fact, it was necessary that the Word be given to us, because otherwise, the noetic effects of sin would not allow us to correctly interpret creation as it truly is (Rom. 1:18). The *horizontal* is the worship of creation, the sinful man's default orientation due to the fall.

With this in mind, we can say that every worldview has a *structure*, that being its network of presuppositions or preconceptions (the beliefs brought to the table), and that it has a *direction*, its religious orientation. The term "worldview" must therefore be understood in that sense, structurally and directionally. And so, when I use the term "religious worldview", I am simply emphasizing its religious orientation so that it is not for-gotten, or worse, so that no one might think there can be such a thing as a religiously *neutral* worldview. There is no such thing.

Herman Dooyeweerd, the 20th century Dutch Christian philosopher, explained in his *magnum opus* of several volumes, *A New Critique of Theoretical Thought*, that there can be no such thing as a "religiously neu-tral starting point." And while the point he made was in reference to theoretical thought, or simply put, scholarship, such as philosophy, the sciences, human-ities, etc., it is a biblical principle that extends to every area of human activity. Bahnsen, a student of Van Til who has since gone to be with the Lord, called this the "myth of neutrality." This is likewise affirmed by Frame and Schaeffer, two other students of Van Til. And while these aforementioned concepts were articu-lated by these wise, godly men, they did not *originate* from them. Instead, they are *rooted in Scriptural truth*. They were simply granted the wisdom to extrapolate and teach these God-given truths.

Everyone, therefore, has a worldview, *a network of presuppositions or preconceptions concerning reali-ty, knowledge, and morality*, and that worldview is *re-ligious* in nature. And while there may be an almost endless number of worldviews in terms of the content of its structure (think of how varied personal beliefs can be from one person to another, e.g., atheist, Mus-lim, Jehovah's Witness, Mormon, cultural Marxist, and within those camps themselves, etc.), there are only *two* religious orientations. In philosophical, academic terms, these are (1) *Anastatic* and (2) *Apostatic*. In more simpler terms, these are (1) Creator-worship and (2) creation-worship. The *Anastatic*, or Creator-worship, is the true worship of God. Whereas the *Apostatic*, or creation-worship, is apostasy—that is to say, a falling away from the true worship, and therefore, idolatry.[2] Any worldview that is not aligned with the worldview taught by the Scriptures is *apostatic*. And what I mean by that is, if a person's worldview does not align with, say, what Scripture teaches concerning the origin of the cosmos and human life, and posits instead naturalism and evolutionism, that worldview is then *apostatic*. If a person's worldview denies the existence or the character and nature of God that is revealed in Scripture, then that worldview is *apostatic*. What we happen to believe as Christians, as reformed Baptists, for example, is *anastatic*, because we have sought to reform and align our respective worldviews with that of Scripture. And while I translate the term to mean "Creator-worship", Dooyeweerd uses this term *anastasis* to mean "standing in the truth."

Could there be more than one *true* worldview? The answer to that question is no. There can only be a singular true worldview when we consider that a world-

2. J. Glenn Friesen, "Anastasis", Christian Nondualism. Accessed October 7, 2021, https://jgfriesen.wordpress.com/glossary/anastasis/.

view is that unifying framework from which we can understand and interpret the world. How do we account for minor differences between respective Christians then? Whether we refer to Anglicans, Baptist, Presbyterians, etc., not in terms of their doctrine, but in terms of their understanding of the world in light of Scripture? We can explain those differences by simply stating that there is one singular, *true* worldview, and that every believer does not 100% align with that true worldview, but does *for most of it*, and as we continue to grow in our knowledge of God and His creation, ideally, the *more aligned we become* with the true singular worldview. We might put it this way, we agree on many of the basic essentials, the *nucleus* per se, but we are still aligning with the *peripherals*. You might call it an on-going reformation of our thought towards the formulation of a distinctly biblical (that is to say, biblically accurate) *philosophy of life*. That is how Van Til termed the Christian "worldview", as a Christian philosophy of life.

### Dooyeweerd's "Philosophy of the Law-Idea"

In terms of formulating or articulating a distinctly biblical, or *Christian* worldview, I much appreciate Dooyeweerd's contribution here with his "Philosophy of the Law-Idea." I am not going to delve too deeply into Dooyeweerd's reformational philosophy, but I will say this: Dooyeweerd taught that all of creation operates as a response to God's law

Herman Dooyeweerd (1894-1977), Portrait, c. 1930.

(e.g., God spoke, and the world came into being). And that it is God's law over creation that operates as the dividing line between Creator and creation. Put another way, we could say that God's law *is* the distinction between Creator and creation. Now, what law am I referring to? The term "creational" law can be referred to here. And being a polymath genius, and drawing from reformed principles and the influence of the Dutch theologian and statesman Abraham Kuyper (1837–1920), who taught the biblical notion of sphere sovereignty (I'll explain that shortly), Dooyeweerd taught that God's creational law can be broken down into fifteen categories, or modalities. I prefer to call them "law-spheres", which means that there are certain laws which govern certain jurisdictions in creation.

First, a brief word on "sphere sovereignty" by Kuyper: Sphere sovereignty is the idea that different areas of life, like family, government, education, and church, each have their own distinct roles and responsibilities, and should be free to manage their own affairs without interference from the others. Imagine society as a soccer field where different teams (spheres) play their own games by their rules; they interact but don't control each other. Kuyper believed that by keeping these spheres separate, society would function more harmoniously, as each sphere could focus on what it does best without overstepping its boundaries. And all of these spheres are subject to the Lordship of Christ. The concept of sphere sovereignty is considered a biblical notion because it reflects the idea that God created various aspects of life with distinct purposes and authorities, similar to how different parts of a body have different functions but work together. For example, in the Bible, the roles of family, church, and government are outlined separately, suggesting that each has its unique duties and responsibilities given by God. Romans 13 talks about respecting governing authorities, Ephesians 5 and 6 discuss family roles, and various passages address the role of the church. Kuyper's idea is like saying God designed a world where different areas of life are like puzzle pieces that fit together, each playing a special role in the bigger picture of how society works, showing harmony and balance. This inspired Dooyeweerd in developing his unifying framework for understanding the world, and the development of his fifteen law-spheres.

The way that Dooyeweerd ordered his fifteen law-spheres was from the most basic to the most complex. I am going to provide an example of how we can understand these law-spheres, but first, let me first show you what those fifteen law-spheres actually *are*.

From most basic to the most complex, these are the fifteen law-spheres:

> You have the (i) arithmetical (or numerical); then you have the (ii) spatial (or geometrical), which presupposes the arithmetical; then you have the (iii) kinematic (or motion), which presupposes the two law-spheres before it (the arithmetical and spatial); then you have the (iv) physical (or physics); then the (v) biotic (or biological); then the (vi) psychical (or psychological); then the (vii) analytical; then the (viii) historical; then the (ix) lingual; then the (x) social; then the (xi) economic; then the (xii) aesthetic (which includes the arts); then the (xiii) juridical; then the (xiv) ethical; and finally the (xv) pistical (or faith). See Figure 1.1.

It should be noted that some laws do not *directly* govern over certain aspects of creation. For example, while the arithmetical up to the physical laws govern over things like rocks, sand, and dirt, etc., the same cannot be said concerning the biotic and psychical, be-

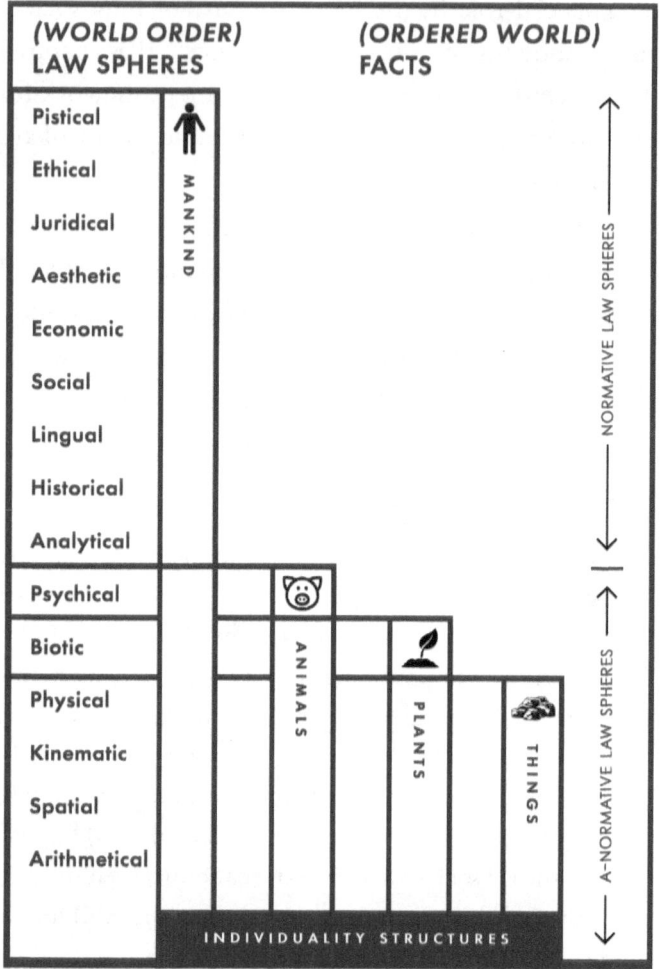

Figure 1.1

cause such things as rocks, sand, and dirt are not *living* things. These non-living things do not operate under the higher law-spheres, they might be involved in some way, as we will see in a later illustration, but they do not directly operate under them. The biotic and all law-spheres below itself certainly govern plants (or vegetation), because plants *are* living things, but not the psychical law-sphere and those above it because plants are not *conscientious* entities. Animals are, but they can only operate as far up as the psychical law-sphere. The only living entity that can operate above the psychical, and which *all* the law-spheres directly govern over, are human beings. Human beings directly engage in economics, in law, in arts, in faith, etc., the same cannot be said of living creatures that are beneath humanity. We might say that this is illustrative of the fact that man is created in the image of God. There is certainly truth to that. Now, as I refer to "non-living things" (such as rock, sand, and dirt), and then plants, animals, and human beings as "living things", Dooyeweerd referred to these as "individuality structures." We do not have to delve any deeper into this, but I mention this so you can understand the table of the fifteen law spheres (see Figure 1.1). Let me also add one more thing, you will notice that according to the table, the six most basic law-spheres are "a-normative", while all the law-spheres above the sixth (the sixth being the psychical) are "normative." Dooyeweerd taught that the laws in the first six law-spheres are inviolable. You cannot violate the laws of the arithmetical (or numerical), or the laws of the spatial (or geometric), or the laws of the kinematic (or motion), etc. However, from the analytical (or logical) up to the pistical (or faith), these creational laws *can* be violated. And they often *are* violated because of the fall of man into sin. We can understand it this way, perfect compliance with the entirety of the law-spheres would be a living out of the good and perfect will of God for creation, *in other words, these laws are the expressed will of God for what creation was supposed to be, how it was supposed to operate.* What might be an example of such a deviation from God's will for creation? Well, some spilled paint on a pile of garbage with flies and maggots all over it might pass off as a work of art in some art shows or museums today, but such a work of "art" violates the laws of aesthetics by not only discarding but also attempting to redefine what is artistic.[3] And who determines what is artistic? Is it not God? Is it not the Creator of all the universe? That is what the terms "a-normative" and "normative" mean, they mean "laws that cannot be violated" and "laws that *can* be violated." Before proceeding further, let me cite for you another illustration that will help you understand how this unifying framework works in regards to our understanding of reality. This illustration is provided by the Dutch philosopher Danie F. M. Strauss (1946–), who presently lives in South Africa. He writes, in his book *Being Human in God's World*:

---

3. The aesthetic scholar Dr. Calvin Seerveld defines "Art" as follows: "Art is the symbolical objectification of some meaning aspect of reality subject to the law of coherence (or allusivity)" as expressed in his *A Christian Critique of Art & Literature* (Toronto, ON.: Toronto Tuppence Press, 1995).

A pile of garbage spray painted over with crawling maggots and flies,
can this reasonably be considered art? It does not have to be beautiful,
but is it meaningful? Modern "art" has become nihilistic.

...( chair possesses four legs (numerical: the interest
of mathematical arithmetic); it is large or small (spatial aspect; mathematical geometry); is a wheelchair or
not (movement aspect: kinematic); it is strong or weak
(physical-chemical aspect); it is usable in human life
(although as biotic object because a chair has no life
– biology studies reality from the biotic aspect); it is
comfortable (sensitive-psychic aspect: psychology); it is
identifiable and distinguishable (analytical aspect: logic); it is culturally formed (historical aspect: historical
science would be interested in, for instance, the historical development of different chair styles); it has a name

(a verbal sign – the sign aspect; general semiotics and linguistics); it is used in the interaction of people (social aspect; sociology); it has a price (economic aspect: economics); it is beautiful or ugly (aesthetic aspect: aesthetics); it belongs to someone who has a subjective right to it (a competence to dispose and enjoy it – juridical aspect: legal science); it is or isn't someone's favourite seat (ethical/love aspect: ethics); and it is reliable – everyone believes that the chair will carry them if they sit on it (faith aspect: viewpoint of theology as science)... Such trust [faith aspect] must not be confused with trusting faith in the religious sense – except of course if someone were to make an idol of the particular chair![4]

For those unfamiliar with philosophy, and most especially with reformational philosophy, this might all seem complex, perhaps even incomprehensible at first, but I really want you to appreciate, for the moment at least, even if you do not understand it all, the *complexity* and the *beauty* of the creation *order*, the *orderliness* of God's handiwork. Now, I know well enough that this is stepping outside of the "theological" nature of these seminars, given that I have stepped into the realm of philosophy, but there is a reason that I share all this with you. I want you to appreciate what Dooyeweerd contributed toward Christian thought: He contributed a distinctly biblical, a distinctly *Christian*, worldview. And the significance of this contribution is made

---

4.   Danie F. M. Strauss, *Being Human in God's World* (Jordan Station, ON.: Paideia Press, 2020), 127-128.

evident when we consider how much of the church's worldview, since the age of the patristics (or church fathers), has been infected and plagued by intrusions of the *antithesis*, that is to say, antithetical worldviews. Dooyeweerd laid this out when surveying the history of Western thought, using the term "ground motives" in his book *Roots of Western Culture* for *the underlying religious motivations (or direction) of man.*[5]

First, a word about what I mean by "antithesis", and then, a summary of the ground-motives presented by Dooyeweerd, which are relevant to our discussion of worldviews.

## Thesis, Antithesis, and Synthesis

The concept of *thesis, antithesis,* and *synthesis* are often associated with the German philosopher Georg Wilhelm Friedrich Hegel (1770-1831), but they originate from a lesser known German philosopher Johann Gottlieb Fichte (1762-1814) who used these terms to describe the process of dialectical reasoning. The American Christian philosopher, H. Evan Runner (1916-2002), however, reframes these terms within a Christian framework or worldview in his book *The Relation of the Bible to Learning*. For Runner, the "thesis" is God's truth revealed, and there is nothing in creation that does not serve as a medium of God's revelation. All of creation is God's medium of general revelation, it is

---

5. See Herman Dooyeweerd, *Roots of Western Culture* (Jordan Station, ON.: Paideia Press, 2012).

what we refer to as God's *creational* revelation. I would go as far as to argue that Dooyeweerd's modal scale of fifteen aspects are informed by God's *creational* revelation. But because of mankind's sin, to be more specific, because of the *noetic* effects of sin, it was necessary that God *re-publish* His thesis, His truth, in the form of the inscripturated Word. This *special* revelation therefore serves as the only authoritative interpretation of God's *creational* revelation, and together the creational and the special presuppose and supplement one another to provide a full picture of the truth of God. And by "truth of God", I do not simply mean what God reveals about Himself, but what He reveals about the world, and our place in it. While it is true that Scripture is not a textbook for any particular discipline or science, as God's inspired Word, it does provide the necessary parameters from which we can rightly understand God's world and from there build up the disciplines and sciences. That is the gist of Runner's book, about developing a Scriptural understanding of academics and politics, but as he also makes clear in his writings, it is not merely a matter of the disciplines, but a matter of human life. As Runner said, "Life is Religion." That is to say, all of human life is *worship*. Which brings me to the next part.

The "antithesis" is that which is contrary to God's "thesis", it is, in other words, the lie. And not just the lie, but the hostile opposition to the truth. As long as we live in a fallen world, the thesis will always be accompanied by the antithesis. The passage of Matthew 13:24-30 comes to mind, concerning the wheat and the tares: there are the people of God and the people of the world, and the two are mixed together in this world until the time comes for the two to be divided. The same can be said of Matthew 13:47-50 concerning the fish that is caught by the fishing net, there are some good and some bad, and the two are separated at the end of the day. Well, that mixing together, that *co-existence* in other words, is the reality of the thesis and antithesis. Van Til, coming back to him again, presupposed this when he wrote concerning "the process of differentiation",[6] which to put into plain words means that, over the course of human history, the thesis and the antithesis will duke it out, the thesis will come out in the end as the thesis, as the victor, while the antithesis will be revealed for what it truly is, the antithesis, and it will be conquered. To put this another way, the truth will be shown to be the truth, and the lie will be shown to be the lie. The people of God will be shown to be people of God's truth, and the world will be shown to be people who are not only lost in their own sin but who are enemies of God set up in hostility against Him. The Christian worldview can thus be referred to as an *articulation* of God's thesis, because it is informed and established upon God's creational and special revelation. Any other worldview can be referred to as an

---

6.  Cornelius Van Til, *Christian Apologetics*, Second edition, ed. William Edgar (Phillipsburg, NJ.: P&R Books, 2003), 68.

articulation of the antithesis. There is one more thing to be said here, and this is regarding the "synthesis."

If there is the thesis (the truth), and then there is the antithesis (the lie), then there is the synthesis which is the attempted combination (or synthesis) of the truth with the lie which in truth becomes another antithesis. What might be an example? When the medieval scholastics of the Roman Catholic church synthesized Scriptural truth with the antithetical philosophies of the ancient Greek philosophers, what they produced, that being "scholasticism", was a synthesis, or a *new* antithesis. It is a synthesis because we have the truth being conjoined with the lie, or with the error, and the end-product is never another "truth" or thesis, it will always be another "antithesis", another lie, that simply *looks* like the truth. What might be another more contemporary example? Theistic evolution is one, where the Scriptural truth of God creating all things is synthesized with Darwinian evolution, producing theistic evolution, which is the belief that all living things (and perhaps even all created non-living things) evolved through the guided hand of God. James K. A. Smith, for example, taught such a synthesis, which has begun to take prominence amongst many reformed believers. Consider what he wrote in his contribution to the book *Evolution and the Fall* concerning the events of Genesis 1 to 3:

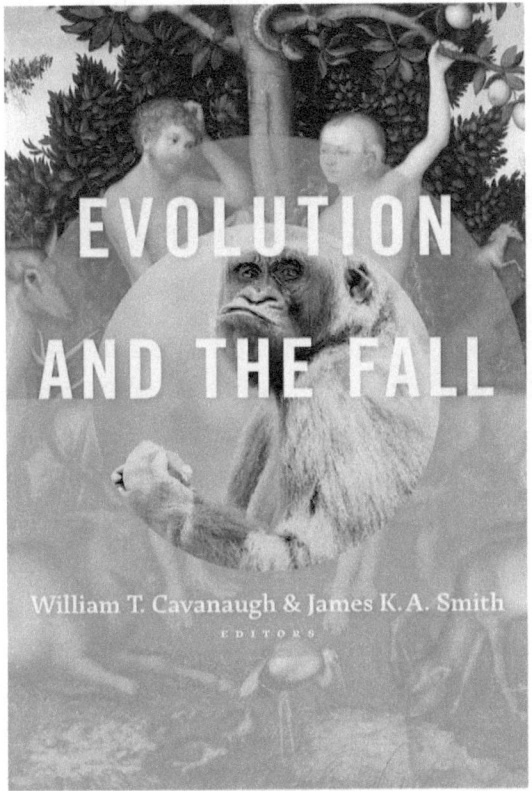

*Evolution and the Fall*, edited by William T. Cavanaugh and James K. A. Smith, is an adequate example of the Thesis being synthesized with the Antithesis in order to produce a Synthesis, which is really a new Antithesis.

From out of this [evolutionary] process there emerges [over a period of millions of years] a population of hominids who have evolved as cultural animals with emerging social systems, and it is this early population (of, say, 10,000) that constitutes our early ancestors [that is, they constitute our understanding of who Adam and Eve are]. When such a population [of animals] has evolved to the point of exhibiting features of emergent consciousness, relational aptitude, and mechanisms of will – in short, when these hominids have evolved to the point of exhibiting moral capabilities – our creating God "elects" this population as his covenant people. The "creation" of humanity, on this picture, is the first election – the first of many (Noah, Abraham, Jacob, et al.)...[7]

Smith, in creating and articulating this synthesis is actually propagating the antithesis. If you get the gist now, a worldview either articulates and reflects the thesis, or it is the antithesis; and when attempts are made to syncretize the thesis with the antithesis, the synthesis it produces is another new antithesis. It is new in one sense, in terms of its articulation and formulation, but it is old in another sense in that it remains antithetical to God's truth. Runner helped me to understand that the development of a biblical worldview is the attempt to faithfully articulate and reflect the published (creational revelation) and re-published (scriptural revelation) thesis of God.

### Ground-Motives & Worldviews

Now, as it concerns "ground-motives", Dooyeweerd was able to identify four ground-motives that have shaped and presently underpin Western thought and culture. These are the four:

---

7. W. T. Cavanaugh and James K. A. Smith, *Evolution and the Fall* (Grand Rapids, MI: Eerdmans, 2017), 61.

1. The Greek Ground-Motive of *Form* and *Matter*
2. The *Nature-Grace* Ground-Motive
3. The *Creation-Fall-Redemption* Ground Motive
4. The *Nature-Freedom* Ground Motive

I explain more in my book *Towards a Christian Understanding*, but for a more in-depth understanding, you can go straight to the source by reading Dooyeweerd's *The Roots of Western Culture*. In the meantime, I will provide a brief summary of the four, prefaced with a word about what Dooyeweerd actually meant by the term "ground-motive": Think of a ground-motive like the main theme of a book or movie, it is the big idea or main force that drives everything forward and shapes how the story unfolds. In real life, ground-motives are like the big, underlying ideas that guide how people think, make decisions, and see the world. They can be likened to hidden rules or themes that influence our beliefs, actions, and the way we understand everything around us. Ground-motives are what gives rise to worldviews.

Now, the first ground-motive begins with the Greeks—because theoretical or philosophical thinking at this level (in terms of a "worldview") does not find its origin earlier than the Greek philosophers. The Greek ground-motive is that of Form and Matter:

Originating from ancient Greek philosophy, particularly from thinkers like Plato and Aristotle, this ground-motive involves the dualism between the ideal

"Plato's Academy mosaic" from the Villa of T. Siminius Stephanus in Pompeii, first century AD.

(form) and the sensory (matter), where the ideal is considered superior and more real than the sensory world, which is seen as a mere shadow or reflection of the idea. If there is a skinny and starving horse, for example, we know that the creature is a horse and that the creature is far from being an ideal horse because somewhere in the world of forms there is a perfect horse, the essence of a horse. And we all *have* this notion because we originated from the world of forms but we are presently trapped in the world of matter in our fleshly bodies (this is why the Greeks perceived the physical body as the prison of the soul, something many Christians believe thanks to the synthesis that followed after this ground-motive). To put this ground-motive plainly, there are two planes to reality: the plane of matter, and the plane of forms, and the plane of matter is where we happen to presently live. And though this plane is a shadow of the ideal plane of the forms, the two can never be reconciled because this world resists being shaped according to the ideal plane of the forms. This is why the soul yearns for the plane or realm of the forms and why Socrates, for example, welcomed death instead of opting to save his own life. There is not much else for me to say here other than to re-iterate that this is an apostate way of seeing the world, and a product of fallen man's thinking.

Then what follows, in the history of Western thought, is the Nature-Grace ground-motive: Emerging in the Middle Ages, this ground-motive reflects the Roman Catholic scholastic *synthesis* of Christian theology with Greek philosophy, particularly through the work of Thomas Aquinas. This ground-motive introduces a distinction between the supernatural realm of grace (associated with God, salvation, and the church) and the natural world. In this dualism, the realm or plane of grace is considered higher and more important than the realm or plane of nature. To put it simply, this is the sacred-secular divide that many Christians have adopted, what we might call the *modern* scholastic position, which (1) regards certain things as sacred and informed by Scripture, and then (2) other things that are secular and informed by natural reason. This *synthesis* is the attempted combination of (1) the knowledge rooted in God's revelation with (2) the knowledge of the natural, fallen man. This ground-motive outright *denies* God's total sovereignty by implication in terms of the the nature of His reign.

Then we have the protestant reformation that followed—that which was sparked by Martin Luther, and which was carried on by various other reformers: The ground-motive of this protestant reformation was that of Creation-Fall-Redemption, it was, in fact, *central* to the Reformation movement. This ground-motive emphasized the biblical narrative and the sovereignty of God over *all* of creation. According to this ground-motive, all of creation was initially good, but was corrupted by the Fall (sin), and is in the process of redemption through Jesus Christ. This ground-motive rejects all dualisms, including that of the Greeks and the Scholastics, and that which would follow later with the Enlightenment. According to this ground-motive, there are no two separate planes of existence, there is one: Creation. And all of creation, though fallen due to sin, will be redeemed and renewed. This ground-motive, therefore, emphasizes the coherence and unity of all aspects of reality under God's sovereignty. It was Dooyeweerd's ground-motive, and it should be ours as well as Christians.

*Der Weimarer Musenhof* (1860); Schiller liest in Tiefurt; *Weimar's Courtyard of the Muses* by Theobald von Oer, a tribute to The Enlightenment and the Weimar Classicism depicting German poets Schiller, Wieland, Herder, and Goethe.

Then we have the Nature-Freedom ground-motive, which arose during the Enlightenment, that rationalist movement of the 17th and 18th century. This ground-motive emphasizes the dichotomy between nature governed by deterministic laws, and human freedom associated with reason and moral autonomy. It reflects the Enlightenment's emphasis on human reason, autonomy, and the scientific understanding of the natural world. To put it simply, there's the world of nature, which follows certain rules (like gravity), and then there's human freedom, where we get to make choices and be creative. It is like saying, "Yes, there are rules we have to follow, but we also get to make our own decisions." There exists, in other words, a tension between the two planes of reality, between nature and freedom, in that nature restricts with all its machinations, while man seeks to be free and struggles against nature's restrictions. Like the dualisms that came before it, the two planes are irreconcilable.

We do not need to go any deeper into Dooyeweerd's conception of the "ground-motives" in order to understand their relevance for our subject matter. It suffices to say that these four ground-motives were what deeply influenced Western thought and culture, and from each of the three apostatic ground-motives there emerged various worldviews. As I had stated earlier, *ground-motives give rise to worldviews.* However, according to Dooyeweerd, the Creation-Fall-Redemption ground-motive, rooted in a biblical perspective, provides a more coherent and unified understanding of reality that avoids the dualisms inherent in the other ground-motives. If you find yourself scratching your head (again) and you are unsure as to how this relates to the concept of "worldview", then let me put it more plainly: Imagine that you are trying to understand why people think and act the way they do, kind of like figuring out the rules of a game that everyone is playing. These four ground-motives are like the big ideas or beliefs that have shaped the way Western cultures see the world and make decisions within it. Understanding these ground-motives, these grand themes or driving forces, is like getting a cheat sheet for why Western cultures think and act the way they do. They show us the big ideas that have been shaping our beliefs, values, and actions over an extended period of time. Just like knowing the rules of a game helps you play better, understanding these ground-motives can help you understand the worldviews around you and why people see things differently. Now, what I had mentioned so far have been the four main ground-motives of *Western* culture, there are in fact *other* ground-motives in what we would call *non-Western* cultures. This includes the pre-Hispanic world, the Oriental, Middle-Eastern, and Australasian cultures, etc. We are not going to get into the specifics today of those other ground-motives, I only mention this to say that ground-motives are everywhere around the world, because they are ultimately the manifestations of the religious state of the heart of man. But to return to the question of "What is a worldview?", in light of all that we have covered so far, including Dooyeweerdian thought, here is perhaps a fuller and more simplified definition provided by James W. Sire from his book *Naming the Elephant: Worldview as a Concept*:

> A worldview is a commitment, a fundamental orientation of the heart, that can be expressed as a story or in a set of presuppositions (assumptions which may be true, partially true or entirely false) which we hold (consciously or subconsciously, consistently or inconsis-

tently) about the basic constitution of reality, and that provides the foundation on which we live and move and have our being.[8]

Let me now make this more relatable by making reference to our present cultural moment.

## Surveying Canadian, Western Culture

I have been trying to define several terms and concepts in such a way that it can be understandable for those who have not had exposure to philosophy before, however, there is one term that needs some further elaboration, the term "culture." What is culture? Culture can be defined as *the religion of the people externalized*. What do I mean by that? Well, culture in this sense is, first of all, *communal*. You cannot have "culture" if you only have a single individual and no one else to partake in it. A married couple can cultivate a culture in their own home, the same is true if they have children. So, firstly, we understand culture to be a *communal* activity. Furthermore, culture is the by-product of man's interaction with creation, either with his neighbour or with creation in general; however he chooses to interact will cultivate and produce some form of culture. So far so good? Consider that the command given to Adam to exercise dominion and multiple and fill the earth, which implied cultivating creation into a godly civilization, was not given *until* Eve had been created (Gen.

---

8. James W. Sire, *Naming the Elephant: Worldview as a Concept* (Downers Grove, IL.: InterVarsity Press, 2004), 122.

1:26-28). Okay, now, remember what Runner had said? Runner had said that "Life is Religion", which means, everything we do is an expression of worship. And this is affirmed by the apostle Paul in the first chapter of his letter to the Romans. We are either Creator-worshippers, or creation-worshippers. This fact is also attested in several other passages in the New Testament, such as:

> So, whether you eat or drink, or whatever you do, do all to the glory of God (1 Cor. 10:31).

> And whatever you do, in word or deed, do it all in the name of the Lord Jesus, giving thanks to God the Father through Him (Col. 3:17).

> Whatever you do, work heartily, as for the Lord and not for men, knowing that from the Lord you will receive the inheritance as your reward. You are serving the Lord Christ (Col. 3:23-24).

These are passages indicative of worshipping the Creator, but you get the point. Culture, being the product of man's interaction with creation, is *religious* in nature; culture is either in worship of God or in worship of creation. Now, let me further simplify this for you by explaining the general anatomy of culture. Culture can be said to consist of three layers: the nucleus, the middle layer, and the surface layer. We always see the surface layer, and very few times do we dig down to the middle layer, and rarely (if we want to be honest about our practical thinking patterns) do we dig down to the nucleus. The surface layer is the behaviour of the people, what they do, how they do it, what they produce, etc. This could be anything from getting drunk at the bars, to putting careers before families, to providing better access to abortions, to opening up injection sites for the drug addicted. It does not necessarily have to be negative, it could also be the opening of new schools, the expansion of hospitals, the building of houses, etc. We see a lot of the surface level of our culture, and it does us no good to isolate one aspect of the surface layer without taking into consideration the broader cultural behaviours.

What then lies below the surface layer? The middle layer, which can be said to be the values of the people. What do they value? Do they value personal freedom? Radical autonomy? We might say, what do they value over other values? Personal freedom over the sanctity of life? Wealth over families? Progressivism over the moral safety and integrity of families? We can be very general in one sense and say that the dominating value of this fallen world is to be like gods, to be radically autonomous in other words, which means to be independent from God in every respect and to be law unto oneself, to call the shots, to make the rules, etc. The impending collapse of Western culture is largely because of that. It raises questions as to, who gets to call the shots? The most powerful? The most wealthy? The most intellectual? The least privileged? We can begin to see how Western culture has become that of a *power strug-gle*, because each man thinks they are their own god, if not consciously then *subconsciously*. It was after all the original sin of man, *it is* the root of *all* sin, and it still dwells in the heart of fallen man (Gen. 3:4-5). Why do you think the natural sinful man hates God? Why do you think that in his sinfulness he resents the gospel? Because it means his dethronement. But while we can be general in one sense when we talk about the under-lying values of Western culture, we can also be specific in light of the fact that everyone comes from a different worldview context. And that is the nucleus of a culture: the people's *religious* worldview. Their heart orientation gives rise to their presuppositions or preconceptions of the world, their *worldview* (the nucleus), and their worldview in turn determines their values (the middle layer), and their values are manifested and reflected in their behaviours or interactions with creation (the sur-face layer). You can begin to see how culture can be defined as the religion of the people externalized. And by implication, if sinful man is not cultivating creation into a godly civilization, then in his apostasy he is cul-tivating creation into a *godless* civilization.

When we look at Western, Canadian culture, for example, we see just that. The surface layer of our cul-ture rarely reflects Judeao-Christian values; and if it ever does, it is largely because there remains some *vestiges* of what used to be a predominant Christian consensus. For the most part, our culture is godless, and there is

another word that might be used to describe the kind of culture we live in, it is quite *pluralist*. What do I mean by *pluralist*? Or *pluralism*? To state that a culture is *pluralist* means that it consists of various differing religious worldviews, and differing not in the minor sense but quite significantly. We might look at Colombian culture, for example, and not call it "pluralist" in comparison to Canada, because although there may be differing worldviews amongst the people, they do not differ as vastly as does the Canadian context. What do I mean by that? Well, Southern Ontario, for example, can boast of its international representation, and because of this internationalism, the diversity of religious worldviews has inevitably followed. We have Muslims, Hindus, Buddhists, Mormons, Roman Catholics, Jews, Doaism, Shintoism, etc., to such an extent that we are not only perhaps the most international spot in Canada or North America (that latter part is arguable), but we are also the most *religiously* diverse spot. St. Catharines, for example, happens to have a mosque, Masjid Noor, on Geneva Street. Niagara Falls boasts of the elaborate Buddhist temple on River Road, called the Ten Thousand Buddhas. Brampton is erecting a 55-foot-tall statue of a Hindu deity. You also have the elaborate Hindu Sridurka Hindu Temple in Toronto.[9] I have not even mentioned the Sikhs, and believe me, there is a significant Sikh population in Southern Ontario. This is all just scratching the surface—you would be surprised just how many mosques, Hindu, Buddhist and Sikh temples, and shrines are spread out across the whole country. You get my point: Western, Canadian culture is pluralist. And because it is pluralist, you have people from such differing religious worldviews, various *non-Western* worldviews (in the sense that such worldviews did not emerge *natively* from Western thought), participating in the cultivation of culture. This makes the work of deconstructing and analyzing the underlying ideologies (or worldviews) of our culture slightly more challenging, as Sire writes:

> Without this knowledge [of worldviews] we are like a diver caught in the tentacles of an octopus. We chop off one tentacle that has us in its clutches, only to find ourselves in the grip of another... Worldview analysis brings the large picture into focus. It illuminates the heart of the matter.[10]

9   See "The Abode of Goddess Durga in North America", *Durka*. Accessed April 03, 2024, https://www.durka.com/

10. James W. Sire, *Naming the Elephant: Worldview as a Concept* (Downers Grove, IL.: InterVarsity Press, 2004), 138.

Thus, by attaining a basic comprehension of the concept of "worldviews", we will be better equipped to not only expose the falsity of these apostate worldviews but to also attest of the *true* Christian worldview. And that brings me to our next and final section: pulling the rug from underneath apostate religious worldviews.

## The Apologetic Method

How do we deconstruct an apostate religious worldview without having to be an expert of said worldview? The notion we get sometimes, particularly within apologetic and philosophic circles, is that we have to *master* the beliefs of the unbelievers we witness to and interact with. While that is not true and should not be required of anyone, it does not hurt to educate ourselves as to what our neighbours *do* believe. The passage of 1 Corinthians 9:19-23 comes to mind, where Paul states to the Corinthians:

> [19] For though I am free from all, I have made myself a servant to all, that I might win more of them. [20] To the Jews I became as a Jew, in order to win Jews. To those under the law I became as one under the law (though not being myself under the law) that I might win those under the law. [21] To those outside the law I became as one outside the law (not being outside the law of God but under the law of Christ) that I might win those outside the law. [22] To the weak I became weak, that I might win the weak. I have become all things to all people, that by all means I might save some. [23] I do it all for the sake of the gospel, that I may share with them in its blessings.

Of course, that does not mean that we are to become Muslims ourselves, or Hindus, or atheists, *but we are to familiarize ourselves with what they believe*, with what they value, in order that we might communicate at a level that they can understand when we testify of the truth of the Christian worldview. The apostle Paul, of course, speaks of the "gospel" in this verse, and while sometimes we do not have much time to share all the background information pertaining to the gospel message, if we can, we *should* communicate not only the gospel message but the worldview from which the gospel is made known to us. In other words, the gospel must be preached from within its Christian worldview, because otherwise it will be distorted and misinterpreted by the listener. The Hindu, for example, may take Jesus and add Him to his many other gods. The Buddhist might treat Jesus as another Buddha. And the atheist may relegate Him to just another moral teacher. How can we communicate this clearly?

Well, Scripture provides us with the wisdom as to how to go about this: A proverbial principle for such situations is given to us in Proverbs 26:4-5, and it is exposited and applied in great detail by the apologist Bahnsen in his book *Pushing the Antithesis*.[11] The text reads:

> [4] Answer not a fool according to his folly, lest you be like him yourself. [5] Answer a fool according to his folly, lest

11. Greg L. Bahnsen, *Pushing the Antithesis*, ed. Gary DeMar (USA: American Vision, 2007).

he be wise in his own eyes.

While the two verses together may seem to be contradictory, they are not; they are instead *complimentary*. Let me explain within this apologetic context: When you engage with someone's worldview, according to verse 4, you are *not* to adopt the presuppositions or preconceptions of the unbeliever in order to make a positive case for the truth. *You cannot, in other words, stand upon the lie in order to lead the unbeliever to the truth.* If you attempt to do so, you will be just like the fool himself, lost in his vain, darkened, and fallen thought. What might be an example? Well, I share this story often regarding my debates with an old high school classmate. His name was Enrique, he was from Nicaragua, and he was also an atheist. He was not one of those atheists who shunned the idea of God, but he was one of those atheists who found great pleasure in debating and emerging the victor. I did not know any better back then, I had only just stumbled upon apologetics, and I was still raw and green like a tomato in my understanding of the truth. His challenge to me, which was continual and constant, was to demonstrate the truth of the Christian God without making any reference to Scripture, and to pretend that Scripture did not even exist. I took him up on that challenge because I thought that by being religiously "neutral" I could still lead him to the truth. I do not know how many times I tried, but I tried several times and never emerged the victor. No matter how hard I tried, no matter what I came up with, I could never lead him from his fallen, apostate thought to the truth of God. He had me discard the inscripturated Word of God in my efforts to make a positive case for the Christian God. As Proverbs 26:4 states, I became like him, like a fool. What should I have done? I should have turned the tables. I should have begun with the wisdom of Proverbs 26:5.

What does verse 5 mean within this context? It means that I can temporarily adopt the presuppositions or preconceptions of the unbeliever in order to demonstrate the futility, the shortfalls, the impossibility of his own worldview. I would be making, in other words, a *negative* case for his worldview. And by doing so, I would not allow him to appear wise in his own eyes, and neither would I appear to be the fool with him. I would have left him *without excuse* for his unbelief. In those debates, I should have asked Enrique how he could possibly account for the intelligibility of the universe without the God of Scripture. I should have asked if he could justify the origin of natural laws in a universe that supposedly emerged from chaos and which, by implication, should operate under the governance of random chance. How could laws, which are constant, predictable, and discernible, operate in such an unstable, unpredictable, and indiscernible universe? The atheist's presuppositions *do not align* with the way he lives and thinks. Instead, he presupposes what the Christian worldview teaches. It is with this revealing fact that Van Til states that the unbeliever is like a child who sits upon his father's lap in order to slap his father across the face. Such an insult, such a demonstration of disrespect, is only possible if the child is held up by the father.[12] That is what the unbeliever does, he borrows the capital of the Christian worldview, the foundational truths of the Christian worldview which allow for an intelligible universe, in order to build his antithetical worldview on top. That is, in fact, what the lie does, the lie lifts off the launchpad of truth, for without the truth, the lie could not be. Remember what I had said earlier, there can be no antithesis if there is no thesis, but because there is a thesis, there is the antithesis. Of course, we are waiting for the day when the antithesis will be done away with altogether. But until then, we have to wrestle with the antithesis.

What might be an example of this borrowing of capital? Well, consider Stephen Hawking (1942–2018), the famous physicist who contributed to our knowledge of black holes and the laws of physics. Hawking, like other scientists, was in search of some unifying theory or framework that would explain the universe, and he believed it was through the lens of physics, or the physical aspect. In his book, *A Brief History of Time*, he writes: "The eventual goal of science is to provide a single theory that describes the whole universe."[13] What

---

12. Cornelius Van Til, *The Case for Calvinism* (P&R Publishing, 1963), 147-148.

13. Stephen Hawking, *A Brief History of Time* (New York, NY.: Bantam Books, 1988), Loc. 240, Kindle edition.

NASA StarChild image of Stephen Hawking, the cosmologist and divulging scientist, who was elected a member of the Royal Society in 1974.

Hawking had attempted was to reduce reality to a singular aspect, in contrast to the multi-aspectual framework provided by Dooyeweerd. Hawking was essentially *deifying* the physical aspect, because to him, the laws of physics were *divine* given that he believed that they had given *existence* to the universe. You can see how an atheistic worldview is theistic in some form or another. It cannot actually remove the object of man's worship, merely substitute it. Well, Hawking's quest came to an end when he realized that the physical aspect cannot provide an account for everything, there were limits to what the discipline could do. That quest was called "The Theory of Everything", and there are several who persist under that false belief. But what these men do is adopt physical laws, that is to say, creational laws which were established by God, and attempt to use these laws to explain away God's existence. They borrow capital from the Christian worldview, from the *thesis*, in order to try to establish the lie. And this trend will continue so for as long as we live in this fallen world. Why? Because mankind, under the noetic effects of the fall, cannot help but absolutize (and thus idolatrize) some aspect of God's creation instead of turning to the One who created the heavens and the earth and in Whom all things hold together (Rom. 1:18-25; Col. 1:17).

What might be another example? Well, a few years ago, the atheist Richard Dawkins (1941–) condemned the massacres committed by ISIS. This is another example of an unbeliever borrowing capital from the Christian worldview in order to make a moral judgment that otherwise would be impossible from a consistently atheistic worldview. If Dawkins was consistent with his atheistic presuppositions or preconceptions, then his moral judgment would be meaningless. As a matter of fact, the massacres carried out by ISIS would be meaningless. We would not be able to call such acts of terror evil, nor would we have any justification for our indignation or moral outrage. At the end of the day, we are nothing more than biological scum dancing to our DNA. One day we are here, the next we no longer are, and there is no overarching meaning to the universe or to our lives. Dawkins, if he was a consistent atheist, should have said nothing, because his atheism requires him to be totally indifferent to morality, to ethics, to injustice, etc. We, however, *can* condemn such acts as evil, we *can* justify our righteous indignation, because we believe in a God who created the universe, we believe in a God who gave us His law, and by God's law we can make moral judgments, by God's law we can identify what is good and what is evil. The atheist presupposes God's law in his living and thinking, even though his professed worldview contradicts it. He cannot help but borrow capital from the Christian worldview, because only from the Christian worldview can we make sense of such things.

Most of the examples I have given are in relation to atheism, but atheism is not the only worldview we engage with in our Western, Canadian context. Remember how I had mentioned how a *pluralist* culture can be challenging to deconstruct and analyze? Well, there is a way to help simplify the cultural worldview landscape:

Do you remember when I had earlier mentioned that there was a Creator-creation distinction? That the law of God served as that Creator-creation distinction? Well, let me elaborate on that because it is immediately relevant to our quest for simplification. The Christian thinker Peter Jones, in his book *One or Two: Seeing a World of Difference*, explains that there are really only *two* worldviews, in the same way that there are only *two* religious orientations (vertical worship of God, and horizontal worship of creation).[14] There is the *One-ist* worldview, in which there is no Creator-creation distinction, and then there is the *Two-ist* worldview, which is the Christian worldview, because there *is* a Creator-creation distinction. This is something we can explore in greater depth at a future time, but for now, we can simply say that those whom we engage with missionally, those who are lost in their sin and therefore apostate in their living and thinking, hold to a *One-ist* worldview. The atheist is no exception, nor the agnostic, because by dismissing the God of Scripture, they deify something else in His place, and that something else is something *in creation*. And even if they do not care whether God exists or not (thinking of the agnostic in this case), something else in their life is treated and regarded as an ultimate in God's place. You can see then that just because a worldview is claimed to be *irreligious*, it is still *religious* in nature because man is a *religious being*. Now, for the sake of time, let us take a look at just *one* other worldview that is overtly religious: Hinduism.

---

14. Peter Jones, *One or Two: Seeing a World of Difference* (USA: Main Entry Editions, 2010).; See also "Only Two Religions", *Ligonier*. Accessed Sept. 15, 2023, https://www.ligonier.org/learn/series/only-two-religions/.

Without detailing all of the primary tenets of Hinduism, it suffices to know that Hinduism, though it appears to be a polytheistic worldview (that is to say, a worldview that boasts multiple gods, in Hinduism's case, *millions* and *millions* of gods) it is actually a pantheistic worldview. In what sense? In the sense that Hinduism teaches that all things, including the gods, are extensions of the impersonal god called *Brahman*. In its simplest form, we could say that, according to Hinduism, all is god and god is all. That is what we call "pantheism." And this overtly pantheistic worldview is a *One-ist* worldview because there does not exist a Creator-creation distinction. Some claim that there is a distinction because there is the illusory world we live in and then there is Brahman, but because we are nothing more than extensions of Brahman, and therefore all divine, that means that there can be no Creator-creation distinction. What are the implications of this worldview? Well, if a Hindu is consistent with his Hinduism, then driving a car over their dog should not be a problem, right? After all, what we have is a person, who is an extension of Brahman, driving a car, which is also an extension of Brahman, driving over a dog, which is also an extension of Brahman. They would have no right to be upset about what just happened. They would have to take it up with Brahman, but they are Brahman too, so how do they make sense of this? Unless, they have been borrowing from the Christian worldview subconsciously! Yes, that can be true even if they have not been exposed to Christianity before. They are still human beings created in the image of God, and they live in the world God created, and therefore they cannot help but presuppose the truth in their living and thinking even though they profess to have another worldview.

There are several other instances where we could make a *negative* case of Hinduism in order to later make a *positive* case for Christianity. One such instance is the fact that they believe that Brahman is an impersonal god that gives form to all that is, but how can an *impersonal* god give form to or manifest a *personal* being? That is much like the atheist believing that out of chaos you can get order. It makes no sense. Our objective in such discussions, in such dialogues, is to make clear that only from the Christian worldview can we make sense of reality, and the proof of the thesis is simply the impossibility of the contrary.

## Concluding Remarks

We need to wrap up. By now, I have inundated you with so much information, with so many concepts, philosophies, definitions, and to top that, proverbial wisdom to inform our apologetic methodology, that I am going to try to bring a satisfying close to our theological seminar.

With all this information, we might be tempted to think that we are either incompetent, unqualified, or not fit for engaging faithfully and missionally with our culture. If that is what you think, then you need to do away with that thought. The objective of this seminar was not to dump so much information on you that you feel incapable of doing anything right because this may all seem so new to you. No, the objective of this seminar was to challenge you to not only be a people of faith, but a people of critical thinking. For far too long has Christianity been considered in recent years a faith devoid of intellectual prowess. Not every Christian will be the brightest in their thinking, nor are they required to, but every Christian is required to love God with all their hearts, all their minds, all their strength (Mark 12:30-31), and this is not only expressed in spiritual piety, but in everything we do in our created world. How are we putting to use our intellectual faculties? How are we glorifying God with our minds? Are we seeking the renewal of our minds daily in Christ? Or are we allowing our minds to be infected by fallen, apostate thought by permitting it to stagnate and therefore to be vulnerable to the thoughts, ways, and agendas of the world? With sharpened minds we can better understand the world, and not just understand it, but engage with it. Remember, we are called to testify of the gospel—well, that gospel is more than just salvation from our sins and judgment, that gospel is also redemption and renewal extending to all of creation under the Kingship of Christ. We do not merely preach a message of salvation only, we preach the gospel of the kingdom of God.

I cannot think of a more apt way to close our time together than to cite this biblical admonishment, which applies just as much to me as to you. The apostle Paul in his letter to the Romans writes the following: "Do not be conformed to this world, but be transformed by the renewal of your mind, that by testing you may discern what is the will of God, what is good and acceptable and perfect" (Rom. 12:2). May the Spirit of God gift us with wisdom and understanding.

**Recommended Reading:**

*A Christian Critique of Art & Literature* by Calvin G. Seerveld (Toronto Tuppence Press)

*Christian Apologetics* by Cornelius Van Til (P&R Publishing)

*In the Twilight of Western Thought* by Herman Dooyeweerd (Paideia Press)

*Pushing the Antithesis* by Greg L. Bahnsen (American Vision)

*Roots of Western Culture* by Herman Dooyeweerd (Paideia Press)

*The Philosophy of Herman Dooyeweerd* by Danie F. M. Strauss (Paideia Press)

*The Relation of the Bible to Learning* by H. Evan Runner (Paideia Press)

# VI

# THE IMPORTANCE OF WORLDVIEW DEVELOPMENT IN EDUCATION

**Date:** May 3, 2024

**Context:** Ontario Christian Home Educators Connection (OCHEC) Convention

**Setting:** Redeemer University, Ancaster, Ontario, Canada

## Introductory Remarks

FOR THOSE OF YOU who may be new to the OCHEC Convention, and to those of you who have perhaps been before, it will probably be much the same that you have not likely heard of the Cántaro Institute. As a reformed evangelical organization, based in the region of Niagara, we are committed to the advancement of the Christian worldview for the reformation and renewal of the church and culture. Our work consists of: *Inheriting* our protestant tradition, *Informing* the church of the relevance and comprehensiveness of the gospel, and *Inspiring* God's people to explore the depths of God's Word and its diverse applications. This afternoon I have the privilege to speak to you about the importance of Christian worldview development, and particularly in relation to education—because, as I am sure is the case for all of us today, we are all educators, and not just educators, but *Christian* educators, in that the education we provide our children is not secular, nor pagan, but rather rooted in the truth of God's Word.

There is much to be said on this matter, but what I want to bring to the forefront of our attention this afternoon is the *antithesis* in education, and how this relates to our own educational efforts. Now, when I use the term "antithesis", I can mean one of two things. I mean either (i) the "anti-thesis", which is the lie that stands contrary to the truth of God, that being the "Thesis", or (ii) the conflict between the truth and the lie.[1] And I mean it in both ways in the sense that, on the one hand, we will be looking briefly at the general underlying antithesis (the lie) of modern education,

---

1.　H. Evan Runner, *The Relation of the Bible to Learning: The Unionville Lectures* (Jordan Station, ON.: Paideia Press, 2023).

and on the other hand, the contrast from (or conflict with) the thesis (the truth) of Christian education. In the end, I will make it clear just how significant it is that we instill in our children, in *all* our children, a *distinctly* Christian worldview, the lens by which they can understand and interpret the world they live in.

## The Definition of Education

We begin first with what our Western world believes as it relates to education, in a most *general* sense, because otherwise we would need well beyond 45 minutes this afternoon if we wanted to go into all the *particulars*. For the world, that is to say, the fallen societal system of man, **education**, whether employed in the public (including Catholic school systems) or private (privatized schools) spheres, **is the process by which we bring the "growing personality that is to be educated into the best possible relation to its environment."**[2] We don't necessary disagree with this *definition* of education, but we cannot take it at face value when presented from a non-Christian worldview. If we were to accept such a definition, we would have to presuppose what Scripture teaches concerning man as a "personality", that is to say, as a creature created in the image of God, as well as what it teaches concerning our "environment", which is to say, the creation of God and our place in

---

2. Cornelius Van Til, "The Antithesis" in Van Til and L. Berkhof, *Foundations of Christian Education* (Phillipsburg, NJ.: P&R Publishing, 1989), 5.

it. And that is not, of course, what our world presupposes by its definition. Already, as to the definition of education, we can see the *antithesis*, the conflict, at the presuppositional, or worldview level between the non-Christian world and the Christian people of God.

For the non-Christian, as an example, God is not some uncreated, self-sufficient, sovereign Being. No, he has dismissed the God of Christian theism and has instead replaced Him with some *finite* god, in whatever shape or form that may be; a god which came about from the universe, from our *finite* universe. The late astrophysicist Dr. Stephen Hawking (1942-2018) comes to mind, the man who, in spite of his poor health, impressed millions with his genius, but who ultimately fell short from finding the theory of everything (that is to say, the theory to *explain* everything).[3] Hawking attempted to reduce all of reality down to the physical;[4] for Hawking, the laws of physics were *divine*,

---

3.  See Sarah Scoles, "Will Scientists Ever Find A Theory Of Everything?", *Scientific American*. Accessed May 04, 2024, https://www.scientificamerican.com/article/will-scientists-ever-find-a-theory-of-everything/.

4.  "The eventual goal of science is to provide a single theory that describes the whole universe. However, the approach most scientists actually follow is to separate the problem into two parts. First, there are the laws that tell us how the universe changes with time. (If we know what the universe is like at any one time, these physical laws tell us how it will look at any later time.) Second, there is the question of the initial state of the universe.

physics was his god, but prior to his death, he came to the realization that the realm of physics, even considering quantum physics, are altogether too restrictive to account for everything in our universe.[5] They only deal, after all, with one aspect of our reality. Though, of course, for Hawking, to have been able to unlock the theory of everything would have been considered being able to solve "god", and the true god would not be the realm of physics in this case, but Hawking himself, *man* himself. If man can completely and exhaustively comprehend "god", then man is the *true* god. This is at the very root of modern non-Christian education, which is why non-Christian education is *man*-centered, godless and humanistic. What do I mean by that? Well, if man does not have to live for God (because he has supposedly done away with God in his thinking), then he may live for himself! This is in stark contrast to the nature of *Christian education*, which is fundamentally *God*-centered. In other words, Christian education is concerned

---

Some people feel that science should be concerned with only the first part; they regard the question of the initial situation as a matter for metaphysics or religion", Stephen Hawking, *A Brief History in Time* (New York, NY.: Bantam Books, 1988), Loc. 240, Kindle edition.

5.   Stephen Hawking, "Gödel and the end of the universe", *Internet Archive: The Way Back Machine*. Accessed Feb. 5, 2024, https://web.archive.org/web/20200529232552/http://www.hawking.org.uk/godel-and-the-end-of-physics.html/.

with bringing the student, the child, face to face with God. Whereas the Non-Christian wants to bring the student face to face *with the universe*. But because the non-Christian believes that man is surrounded by an absolutely unknowable universe, he is left at best as a being who desperately grasps in the dark, and, as the late Cornelius Van Til (1895-1987) wrote, "except for the little light that his own mind is radiating as a head-light in the mist."[6] This, of course, is not the case with the Christian, because for us, we know that man originally lived under the light of God's revelation, and that today, under (i) Christ, who is our *fact-revelation*, and under (ii) Scripture, which is our *Word-revelation*, man is in principle restored to that true light of God.[7] What do we mean by Christ as "fact-revelation"? That may be a new term for you compared to "Word-revelation." By "fact-revelation", I mean Christ as the *center* of all truth, as the knowledge (epistemological) foundation for *all* truth. This means that Christ, as the *fact-revelation*, is the lens through which all facts must be interpreted, because Christ, who is the ultimate truth, is in Whom all other truths of our created reality are given meaning.

### The Purpose of Education

As to the *purpose* of education, non-Christian education does not have anything of any real substance to say.

---

6.    Van Til, *Foundations of Christian Education*, 3.

7.    Ibid.

Plato's Academy mosaic, made between 100 BCE to 79 AD, shows many Greek philosophers and scholars. Roman mosaic of the 1st century BCE from Pompeii, now at the Museo Nazionale Archeologico, Naples.

Ever since the Enlightenment of the 17th to 18th-century, when the effort was made in earnest to separate education from Christian influence, the whole foray of discussion has been toward *that way* and *the other way*, a mad dash from one end of the spectrum of aspects to another—all desiring at the end of the day some definitive purpose for education but not finding any that appears satisfactory for collective man. For those who had reduced reality to the economical (think Karl Marx), education was to be perceived solely within that economic aspect; for those who reduced reality to the psychical (think Sigmund Freud), education was to be perceived solely within that psychical aspect. The same can be said for those who reduced reality to the physical, the social, the biotic (think Charles Darwin), etc.[8] When surveying the history of Western thought, there has in truth been no real progress made, no final word given, because as long as reality remains an unknowable mystery, then the meaning of reality itself is still up in the air. And if such is the case, what then is the purpose of education? To uncover the meaning of reality? The non-Christian doesn't even know what reality *is*. As Van Til rightly states:

> [Non-Christians] talk of "functional adjustment" to one's environment. But if man does not know the road and drives in the mist, why should he "step on the gas"?[9]

Christian education, however, has a clear vision, a clear *purpose*, and that purpose is in light of man's chief end. As the Westminster Shorter Catechism states: "Man's chief end is to glorify God, and to enjoy him forever" (Cf. Ps. 145).[10] The purpose of education is to bring man face to face with God, His Creator, and to help him understand the significance of all things in relation to God, in order that he might live and glorify

---

8. See Figure 1.1 on page 146.

9. Van Til, *Foundations of Christian Education*, 3.

10. *The Westminster Standards*. Accessed May 03, 2024, https://thewestminsterstandards.com/q1-what-is-the-chief-end-of-man/.

Him and delight in Him forever. In order to fulfill that purpose, Christian education must therefore contain *distinctly* Christian content. What do we mean by that?

## Non-Christian vs. Christian Content

Well, non-Christian education, for example, asserts that whatever man can know, he can know *apart from God*. The human mind, therefore, is not like a light bulb which requires an electrical current in order to shine light, rather, for the non-Christian, the human mind is like an oil lamp with its own oil supply.[11] To put it another way, the human mind is not dependent upon the ultimate, it *is* itself the ultimate, arrogantly self-sufficient. We as Christians, however, hold that everything is dark *without* the light of God's revelation, and therefore, without the light of God's revelation, all we really do is grasp in the dark in search of understanding. Consider, for example, a teacher who teaches virtue in his classroom from a non-Christian worldview. He may refer to the virtue of those who provided refuge to persecuted Jews in World War II, or to the admirable efforts of Mother Teresa to help the poor and the sick, or even the firefighters and policemen who gave their lives saving people during 9/11. The teacher *thinks* he knows what virtue is, he sees it, and yet, because he or she is a non-Christian, when it comes to actually *defining* virtue, when it comes to defending and upholding virtue, it is at that point that

11. Van Til, *Foundations of Christian Education*, 4.

Mushroom cloud above Nagasaki after atomic bombing on August 9, 1945.
Taken from the north west, with newspaper sample piece. Picture by Charles Levy,
U.S. National Archives and Records Administration. Public Domain.

virtue suddenly becomes a *mystery*, for who determines
virtue? If the Nazis had won World War II, would virtue have changed in public opinion? Would what was
once virtuous still be considered virtuous today? What
is virtue? What standard do we have for virtue? He or
she does not really know, because at the end of the day,
to know virtue is to know morals, and what are morals
without the law of God? The history of non-Christian

man is an unending cacophony of man-made morals which have never remained constant and absolute. As an atheist once told me, morals must be seen for what they are, products of those who have won the world's wars, which, had the wars gone differently, morality would have been entirely different today. Van Til, on this note, says the following:

> Non-Christian teachers will accordingly sometimes think they really have and know the "facts" and can teach the child all about them, and then again when they see that the "facts" are really in the dark they will give up in utter despair.[12]

That is, of course, *not* our predicament, for as Christians, as Christian *educators*, we know that not a single "fact" of created reality is unknowable when it is under the light of the revelation of God. We can know what virtue is, *truly* know that is; we can know what morality is, we can know any "fact" of discussion and observation, because we are not grasping about in the dark, we have (i) Christ who is our light, and (ii) His Word, which is the only authoritative interpretation of God's creation. This can be said even of the most basic of disciplines, of the most basic of reality's aspects, such as that of the arithmetical (the numerical). For as Van Til writes:

> When you think of two times two as four, you connect this fact with numerical law. And when you connect this

12. Ibid.

fact with numerical law, you must connect numerical law with all law. The question you face, then, is whether law exists in its own right or is an expression of the will and nature of God. Thus the fact that two times two are four enables you to implicate yourself more deeply into the nature and will of God.[13]

These may seem like *basic* distinctions, but they are fundamentally *important* distinctions, because in the non-Christian case, we are talking about children being placed in a vacuum, in the void, in a totally God-*less* place, and expecting a child to grow in their personhood. Of course, the child inevitably *dies*, in the sense that he or she never becomes what he or she was meant to become. Christian education, however, does not place the child in a vacuum, instead, the child is placed face to face with God. And this is because, we do not actually believe that children can grow, *properly grow*, in their personhood unless they are face to face with God, for it is only then that we can hope to see children become the persons they were meant to be, that is to say, according to God's creational intention. Christian education, in other words, gives children the air and food they need to live, to grow, to mature, *to become who God meant them to be as persons, bearing the image of God.* Whereas non-Christian education has sought to do away with divine authority, believing that it all somehow "harms" rather than benefits the child, we in contrast believe that *without divine authority, a*

13. Ibid., 7.

*child cannot live at all.*[14] And by divine authority, we mean God as Creator, and Christ as Redeemer.

In truth, the conflict between non-Christian and Christian education can be reduced to a matter of ultimates: What is the ultimate behind everything? The ultimate that gives *meaning* to everything? For non-Christian education, some aspect of the universe is an ultimate, and that ultimacy was determined by an even greater ultimate, the rationalist mind of man, which in either case—whether we speak of the former or the latter—is still *finite*. For Christian education, however, the Creator God of Scripture is our ultimate, and our ultimate, in contrast to the non-Christian, is an absolute, personal, self-sufficient and infinite Being. When consulting the writings of the Christian philosopher Herman Dooyeweerd (1894-1977),[15] as well as his contemporary Van Til, we find no more ultimate assertion that none of creation can make any sense if it is not in relation to God, and centered around Christ who *is* meaning, just as He is life, since all things were created *through* Him, and *in Him* all things hold together. We cannot, therefore, say that the two underlying worldviews of non-Christian and Christian education differ at perhaps a seventy or ninety percent degree; no, they differ *totally* and *radically*. As Van Til puts it,

---

14. Ibid., 4-5.

15. See Herman Dooyeweerd, *A New Critique of Theoretical Thought*, Vols. I-IV (Jordan Station, ON.: Paideia Press, 2021).

The two different conceptions of God that underlie the two educational theories cover every point on the whole front and cover them before and behind, without and within.[16]

## The Way We Educate

We notice this in the *way* that we educate our children. For example: for the non-Christian program of education, you will notice that there is an almost all-embracing approach of all of the world's philosophies and traditions—I say "almost" because non-Christian programs do in fact *supress* that which works contrary to its agenda (e.g., progressivism, inclusivity, wokeness, etc.) and that which explicitly exposes its falsities (e.g., logical and philosophical inconsistencies and contradictions, etc.). It is as the apostle Paul wrote in Romans 1:18, man suppresses the truth by his unrighteousness. You get what I am trying to say: in non-Christian education, you will often get a hefty dose of Darwinism, Marxism, utilitarianism, progressivism, liberalism, scholasticism, critical race theory, etc., but you will not get much of a *deconstruction*, a "breaking down" of these things in a critical way. The Christian program of education, on the other hand—if it is a *distinctly* Christian education—differs in that it may well cover these things but with a mind of deconstructing and critiquing these things as *antitheses*, that is to say, as various lies believed in and propagated by our world. These are

16. Van Til, *Foundations of Christian Education*, 7.

all examined under the light of Christ and His Word. While the non-Christian program looks to build upon almost everything for the education of the student, the Christian program breaks everything down before it can possibly build up upon the truth.[17] The wisdom of men, in other words, needs to be done away with in order for the wisdom of God to be elevated in the mind of the student.

Put another way, when we speak about the *way* we educate, the distinction between the thesis and the antithesis needs to be made clear, and this is true regardless of what subject or discipline we may explore. If we teach mathematics, for example, then we may speak of the history of mathematics and how, only from a Christian worldview, can we make sense of the underlying mathematical laws, versus how non-Christians are unable to make sense of such mathematical laws even though they recognize and abide by them. If we teach history, we must teach history in light of the grand biblical narrative of creation, fall, and redemption, because only then does history have true objective meaning, whereas for the non-Christian, history is open to interpretation, even re-invention, and made out to be whatever the populace decides. To teach mathematics *Christianly*, as well as to teach history *Christianly*, does not mean using the Bible as our textbook, but rather as the lens through which we see and interpret the world. It is only then that we can teach such disciplines in

---

17. Ibid., 8.

reference to God and His centrality to all truth and meaning.

## The Implications of Non-Christian and Christian Education

We now, of course, need to address the implications of a non-Christian and Christian education. And while what I have covered thus far does indeed touch on the implications, there is still more to consider. When we speak about education as *"the process by which we bring the growing personality that is to be educated into the best possible relation to its environment"*, the non-Christian really has no idea as to the "personality" of man and as to the meaning of his "environment" and its constitution. When we read Romans 1, particularly verses 18 to 27, we read of how there can only be *two* objects of man's worship, that being God our Creator, and God's creation. In his sinfulness, mankind has exchanged his worship of the true Creator God for creation, and by doing so, he abandoned his worldview which consisted of a Creator-creation distinction, and adopted in its place a monistic, One-ist worldview in which the Creator-creation distinction has been blurred to the point of non-existence.[18] By removing the most fundamental of distinctions of reality, that being, the Creator-creation distinction, the non-Christian has reduced his reality to one without distinctions, where the

---

18. See Peter Jones, *One or Two: Seeing a World of Difference* (USA: Main Entry Editions, 2010).

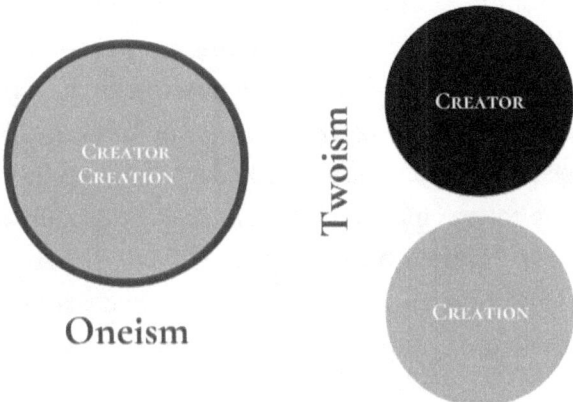

Oneism

Twoism

numbers 1, 2, and 3 are not distinct but one and the same. That is not the case for non-Christians, of course, because they too can do math; and they recognize that there is such a difference as between one apple, two apples, and three apples. But what they end up doing is living in such a way that contradicts their professed worldview, that is to say, living in such a way that presupposes the Creator-creation distinction which they have done away with in their heart's worship. This is the implication of *apostatic* thinking, it is the result of the apostatic state of the heart (by apostatic, I mean a "falling away from the truth", as it is meant biblically).

What is man as a person if the non-Christian has dismissed the One from whom man derived his personhood? Man is not a self-sufficient being, he is a derivative being! Deriving his being from the Creator. In the same way, man is not self-sufficient in his knowledge, being a derivative being, he derives *true* knowledge from the Creator! But because the non-Christian has dismissed God in his thinking, in his confession, in his living, he is left with a puzzle that he cannot solve, the puzzle of the meaning of the universe. How many philosophers and intellectuals have spilled ink looking for the meaning of existence? How many have succeeded in their quest *apart* from God? The fact that the non-Christian world has never reached a consensus speaks volumes as to its failure. As Van Til notes,

> The philosopher of today has given up every attempt to understand the meaning of the whole of reality.[19]

And as the late German philosopher Karl Jaspers (1883-1969) speculated:

> The contemplation of total reality, the idea of knowing so as to understand what total reality, historically and in the present, might be, is a fundamental mistake; the existence of this total reality is itself open to question.[20]

It was this Jaspers, who hailed from Germany in the late nineteenth century, and who would go on to make his contributions in Switzerland in the early twentieth century, that said that education (for the non-Christian) was an effort lacking of all confidence of what it taught, with the inherent human desire that the answer to the meaning of everything would suddenly come

---

19. Van Til, *Foundations of Christian Education*, 11.

20. Karl Jaspers, *Die geistige Situation der Zeit* (*The Intellectual Situation of Our Time*) (Berlin: W. de Gruyter, 1932), 22.

about through the education of the generations. In his own words,

> A generation which has no confidence in itself occupies itself with education, as though here again something could come into being from nothing.[21]

What about non-Christian education makes that most evident? The fact that there is no centrality to non-Christian education, and the lack of centrality, the lack of prioritization, is due to the fact that it knows not its purpose. Whatever purpose non-Christian education claims to have is ultimately contradicted on all fronts by differing philosophies, while at the same time lacking in its philosophical consistency and congruency because it denies the fundamental nature of reality, principally, that we are created by God and in His image, and that we live in His world and before His presence. Non-Christian education is not a mandate fulfilled, it is a social and existential experimentation. Children who are in the hands of modern non-Christian education are nothing more than *social experiments* in the eyes of the West. That is not so the case for Christian education. We know that the purpose of education is to bring man face to face with God, His Creator, and to help him understand the significance of all things in relation to God, in order that he might live and glorify Him and delight in Him forever. *The glorification of God* is man's chief end, and this brings forth

---

21. Ibid., 94.

Karl Jaspers: *Allgemeine Psychopathologie*, first print 1913. The photo may be used
freely for scientific publications, provided the author is credited as "Photo H.-P. Haack",
Antiquarian Dr. Haack Leipzig.

delight, because God was always meant to be created
man's *delight*. Education must *serve* this end, it must
*serve* this purpose, to bring man to that point while
standing upon God's truth and affirming the authority
of the Lordship of Christ. Christian education, therefore, *does* have centrality. Contrary to the disarray of
non-Christian education, we will find that all the dis-

ciplines are not disconnected but rather all intertwined towards bringing glory to the God of Scripture, the God of the heavens and the earth. When contemplating the very nature of Christian education, we see then that it involves more than simply the advancement and communication of knowledge and skill, which is what primarily characterizes non-Christian education. No, Christian education goes well beyond that by cultivating within the student *godly wisdom* and *virtue*. Our children, therefore, are not *encyclopedias-to-be* (as wonderful as that might sound), they are disciples subject to Christ, in Whom all things hold together. And as disciples, they're to learn what it means to worship God in all aspects and spheres of life.

This means that, one day, our children may be *Christian* doctors, *Christian* plumbers, *Christian* engineers, *Christian* scientists, *Christian* politicians, *Christian* cooks, *Christian* architects, *Christian* athletes, *Christian* homemakers, etc.[22] We might ask what makes them so different from their non-Christian colleagues in these respective professions? Structurally-speaking, the work may seem much the same. A doctor who cuts open a patient for surgery is the same whether he is a Christian or not. The same can be said for an athlete who kicks a ball. Or an astronomer who looks out upon the night sky with his telescope. Or a researcher who cracks open

---

22. See Willem J. Ouweneel, *The World is Christ's: A Critique of Two Kingdoms Theology* (Jordan Station, ON.: Paideia Press, 2017).

a book. We all drive cars, we all go to school (whether that be at an institution or some place in the home), we all cook, shop, read, and work, etc. Structurally-speaking, it may all seem much the same. But *directionally-speaking*, that is another matter, and that is what most sets us apart. Everything we do, we do to the glory of God, and everything we do, we do subject to His Word, in obedience to Christ our Lord. And it is our direction, which is determined by the heart, the center of the human person, the *ego*, that gives shape and form to what we do *structurally* in God's created world, in every sphere, in every functional aspect.

## Two Sources of Wisdom: One False, One True

As I work our way towards our conclusion, I wanted to bring Socrates and Christ into our view in order that we can understand the distinction that exists between human and godly wisdom, and therefore, the distinction between non-Christian and Christian education. Or to use the language of King Solomon, with the voice of the *Qohelet* from the Book of Ecclesiastes, the difference between madness/folly and wisdom (Eccl. 1:17).

Socrates, if you are aware of his story, was an ancient philosopher that had a knack for annoying even the most patient and respected philosophers of his day. How exactly did he do this? Well, according to Plato's *Apology*, Socrates went about questioning every philosopher he came across to see whether they really *knew* anything, and he meant, anything with absolute certainty and without a doubt. It was a comedic read for me in my University years, because, in the end, the wisdom he arrived at was that *we do not know anything at all.* If we were to paraphrase Socrates, it was "I know that I know nothing." And that is very much the case for the non-Christian, because though he may claim to know things, even to the extent of building elaborate philosophies, scientific theories, and physical/mechanical structures, when pursuing his underlying worldview and carrying his presuppositions to its logical end, he comes to the conclusion that he does not *truly* know. He may know that 2 + 2 = 4, but he cannot *make sense* of the mathematical law behind it.

Christ, on the other hand, stands in contrast to Socrates in that Christ is the embodiment, the manifestation, the source, and revealer of truth. In John 14:6, Jesus said, "I am the way, and the truth, and the life. No one comes to the Father except through me." The words of Christ are strikingly different than Socrates.

We might put it this way: Socrates can serve as an ideal portrait of the sinful man in his fallen thinking, he knows that he knows nothing, and thus he is aware that he is a walking and talking contradiction (he knows but does not know, such ignorance is the cause of the noetic effects of the Fall). But Christ, the One *through Whom* all things were made, and the One *in Whom* all things hold together, is the revelation of truth, and the *ultimate* authority for truth. His revelation shines light upon the darkness of our world and allows us to see things for what they truly are, to interpret creation in light of God's truth, free from the sinful distortions of man. Socrates can be seen as the pinnacle of man's pretended self-sufficiency, revealing himself to be a fool like all the rest, while Christ is, in fact, the self-sufficient Being, revealing Himself to be the wisdom of God and the One in Whom all things find their meaning. It was the reformational philosopher and minister, Andree Troost (1916-2008), who had the following to say regarding our faith, Christ, and how all things ought to be in reference to Him:

> For in the Christian faith we confess that the totality of all creation was created by God "in Christ" and that the entire "fullness" of creation is not only "through Him" but "in Him," and is also directed to Him, and saved, redeemed and renewed "in Him."[23]

## Concluding Remarks

The objective of our time together this afternoon was not only to help flesh out the difference between non-Christian and Christian education—we all recognize such a distinction given the fact that we have all decided to provide our children a *Christian* education. The objective was also to encourage you to ensure that whatever you teach your children, whether it be history, science, grammar, or phonics, you name it, that

23. Andree Troost, *What is Reformational Philosophy?: An Introduction to the Cosmonomic Philosophy of Herman Dooyeweerd* (Jordan Station, ON.: Paideia Press, 2020), 42.

"Socrate du Louvre", Portrait of Socrates. Marble, Roman artwork (1st century), perhaps a copy of a lost bronze statue made by Lysippos.

it always be in reference to God, and that Christ be at the center of it all. And not just in the delivery of our programs to our children, but in everything we do, whether in the home, at work, with friends, shopping, or at the church. We can now perhaps begin to see just how significant it is that we instill in our children a *distinctly* Christian worldview, a Scriptural lens, with Christ at the center, by which they can understand and interpret the world they live in. It was my dear friend, Ryan Eras, the headmaster of the upcoming Niagara Classical Academy, who said that "Everything we do, we *teach*"—as a matter of fact, we are always teaching, not just by our words, but by what we do, because as I am sure you are all keenly aware, our children see everything we do, *rarely* do they miss anything. And so, to be a teacher, to be a *Christian* teacher, is not something we are and do only during our scheduled programs, it is what we are and do with every breath we breathe. Let us therefore live Christ-centered lives, walking before the face of God, in hope and faith that our children will join us as well. And never losing sight of the purpose of education: *To bring our children face to face with God, their Creator, and to help them understand the significance of all things in relation to God, in order that they might live and glorify Him and delight in Him forever.*

# VII

# THE TEN
# COMMANDMENTS

**Date:**    May 18, 2024
**Context:** The Theological Seminars
**Setting:** Sevilla Chapel, St. Catharines,
          Ontario, Canada

### Introductory Remarks

OVER THE COURSE OF OUR Theological Seminars, we have touched upon two different components of what we might term the Christian "curriculum." We looked at Church History back in January, particularly, the Spanish protestant reformation; and Apologetics in March, though most specifically as it related to religious worldviews. This morning we are going to look at the Bible component, that is to say, the study of the Holy Scriptures; and our particular focus will be on the Law of God, or to be even more precise, the "Ten Commandments"—because to study the Law in its entirety would mean to study the *Torah* in its entirety, and as you can imagine, we do not have the time for such an expansive study, nor is it my intention to expand the scope of our study to such a wide gamut.

For those of you who may be joining us for the first time, the Theological Seminars have been a jointly organized series of studies between Sevilla Chapel and the Cántaro Institute. The Institute was founded in the year 2020, and it was intended to resource the local church with its teachings—and what we are accomplishing here, with our Theological Seminars, is what we hope we can replicate in various other places in the future as the Institute grows in its stature and reach. For those new here and therefore unfamiliar with the Institute, the Cántaro Institute is a reformed evangelical organization committed to the advancement of the Christian worldview for the reformation and renewal of the church and culture. There are three main modes of function of the Institute, and these are to *Inherit*, to *Inform*, and to *Inspire*. In its simplest form, I can summarize these as follows: The Cántaro Institute seeks to fulfill its mission by *embracing* (*inheriting*) our protestant past, *informing* our protestant faith, and *inspiring* the protestant church.

It was not that long ago that we had a conference with Rev. Marcos Peña of the IBSJ, the Iglesia Biblica del Señor Jesucristo, in Toronto, and for those unfamiliar with Rev. Peña, he comes from a church based in the Dominican Republic pastored by Sugel Michelén, a key figure in the unfolding reformation amongst Latin American churches. We hope to have Rev. Peña's lectures available for public viewing in the coming weeks, but in about a month's time we have another conference for Spanish-speakers, this time with Joe Owen of Answers in Genesis (LATAM). In both instances, we have aimed to speak specifically on sensitive cultural issues, such as the family and sexuality, in order to boldly speak truth in an age that has been otherwise characterized by incoherent confusion. If you have not already made arrangements to attend the event on June 15, 2024, we recommend that you do so. Space will be limited. And for those amongst us who are more English-language-inclined, our annual Niagara Conference will be taking place on November 16, 2024 at Reformed Heritage Congregation in Jordan Station. With the theme *Post Tenebras Lux: Light after Darkness*, we will be examining the protestant reformation with speakers such as Dr. Ted Van Raalte of the Canadian Reformed Theological Seminary, Dr. David Robinson of Westminster Chapel, who is also a scholar of ancient church history, and Dr. Brian G. Najapfour, who presently pastors Reformed Heritage Congregation. More information about our events and how to register for future events are available on the Institute's website.

All of this I share with you because I want you to be sensitive to what the Lord has been doing in our midst. He is raising up the church to be a prophetic voice in our culture and to fulfill its call to be salt and light—salt in the sense that we are preventing the rot of sin from progressing any further in its damage of human society, and light in the sense that we are shining the light of Christ in a dark world that has been plunged into futility and desperation. As a church, as a collective people, we need to do more than just gather on Sunday mornings and produce pious-looking Christians. As a church, we are called to march out like an army, carrying the sword of the Word of God, proclaiming the Word of truth, who is both Christ and His written revelation, and commanding all to repent and believe in the Lord Jesus Christ (Heb. 4:12). And we know that this Christian belief, we know that this "faith", is much more than just a privatized spirituality, it is a faith that encompasses all aspects of life, a faith which informs our living and thinking, a faith which brings glory to our God in heaven. We are, therefore, not bearing witness of a hell-fire insurance for those who are perishing, we are bearing witness of a Christian philosophy of life, one which directly touches upon our epistemology (knowledge), our metaphysics (reality), and our ethics (morality). We do not have in mind only the promise of Paradise far beyond our earthly lives, no, we also have in mind right God-fearing living in the here and now, living before the face of God. And for this reason, we have our Theological Seminar this morning, as an opportunity for us to grow in our knowledge of God, and in the development of a distinctly Christian worldview, in order that we might fulfill our part as ambassadors of Christ. Ask yourselves this, What soldier goes to war without training? What soldier enters battle without the right tools? We aim to provide the training *and* the tools for the cultural war we daily wage, a cultural war that is not earthly (that is to say, fleshly), but spiritual, *religious*, a conflict that rages between the *Thesis* of God, the Truth, and the *Antithesis*, the Lie.

That brings us to the subject of the Ten Commandments, as a subtopic of the Bible component of our Christian curriculum, because when we look at that cultural war which the church finds itself inevitably engaged in, it is not a matter of a difference of preferences, but rather, a matter of lawful obedience to the law of God and of cosmic treason. Those who are God's people are on the side of lawful obedience, the result of the Spirit's regenerative work in the hearts of believers, while those who are of the world, those who have embraced the Antithesis, the Lie, are on the side of cosmic treason—they have no respect for the law, instead, they believe themselves to be a law unto themselves.

Now, a word does need to be said about "Law", because a study of the Law makes no sense if we do not understand from which *lens* we are seeing the Law. The "Law" for the Christian is a very different "Law" from that of the unbeliever. For the Christian, we understand "Law" to be God's "Law", it finds its origin in

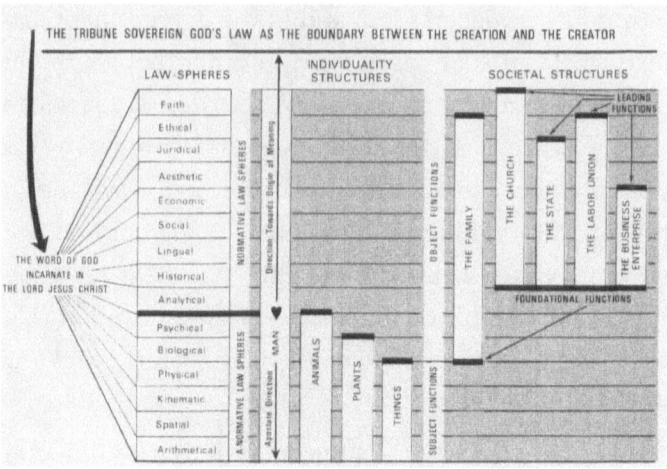

"The Tribune Sovereign God's Law As The Boundary Between The Creation And The Creator"
according to Herman Dooyeweerd, 1960s.

the Law-giver, the Absolute, the Creator of the heavens and the earth. While, for the unbeliever, "Law" is often regarded as a by-product of a non-theistic, self-sufficient cosmos, or as something constructed by man, depending on the circumstance and the one examining it. In truth, there are various differing perspectives of what "Law" is, but so long as they are not understood within the light of God's creational and special revelation, the definition falls short and misses the picture of what "Law" really is. "Law", from a Scriptural standpoint, *is the expressed will of God for His creation.* And "Law" can be divided, for the purposes of our study, into two categories: Creational and Scriptural (or Moral).

## Creational Law

When I speak about "Creational Law", I mean the set

of laws I had made mention of in our last time together, when we talked about "Religious Worldviews." In that seminar, I had touched on reformational philosophy, most particularly the development of a modal scale, or hierarchy of creation law-spheres, developed by the Dutch polymath genius Herman Dooyeweerd (1894-1977). The modal scale, or the table of creational law-spheres, were fifteen in total, beginning with the arithmetical (or numerical), and working our way up to the spatial, the kinematic, the physical, biotic, etc.[1] I am not going to delve into these creational law-spheres today, but if you would like a general introduction to this, I would advise that you pick up a copy of Danie F. M. Strauss' book *The Philosophy of Herman Dooyeweerd* and Willem J. Ouweneel's *Wisdom for Thinkers*. Well, returning to the subject matter at hand, "Creational Law" is not what I have in view here for our study today. However, just so that we correctly understand what I mean by "Creational Law", consider the following illustrative example:

While this is before my time, many of you will remember when, on July 20, 1969, the American Neil Armstrong stepped out of his lunar lander to step foot, for the first time in all human history, on the moon. We know this to be a fact because it is a well documented historical event. But imagine now that Armstrong, instead of wearing his protective space suit, stepped out of the lander in plain civilian clothes. No respirator,

---

1    See Figure 1.1 on page 146.

no solar shielding, no insulation, nothing, just plain clothes. What do you think would have happened to Armstrong? He would have died a most horrific death. Why? Because Armstrong had been removed from the law-environment for which he was created, and being outside of that law-environment, death would be a certainty. The same applies to a fish taken out of water. As the late Christian thinker Cornelius Van Til (1895-1987) put it:

> According to [Christian] theism, man lives and moves and has his being in an atmosphere of the law of God both for his body and for his soul. To live in this atmosphere meant his freedom as it means freedom to a fish to live in its native element.[2]

All "Creational Law" is to be understood as the expressed will of God for creation. "Creational Law", however, is distinct from "Scriptural Law", in that the latter has to do chiefly with how man ought to live in relation to God, His Creator. The former has to do with man's function in relation to his environment. But the two are not severed off from each other as being totally independent and not having the one to do with the other. Man's response to this "Scriptural Law" is manifested in how he lives and functions within the respective spheres of "Creational Law." For example, if man violates the law of "Thou shalt not steal", not only

---

2. Cornelius Van Til, *The Ten Commandments* (Jordan Station, ON.: Cántaro Publications & Paideia Press, 2024), 13.

has he violated God's "Scriptural Law", but this violation is made manifest in his violation of "Creational Law". How so? Well, in the *Juridical* aspect, for example, man would have violated legal laws and regulations that prohibit theft. Theft directly contravenes the legal system's statutes designed to protect property rights. In the *Ethical* aspect, man would have violated the moral norms and ethical principles regarding respect for others' property. Theft is considered morally wrong as it involves dishonesty and a lack of respect for the rights of others. In the *Economic* aspect, man would have violated the principles of fair exchange and stewardship of resources. Theft disrupts the fair distribution and management of resources, impacting the economic balance. In the *Social* aspect, man would have violated the social norms and expectations concerning trust and cooperation. Theft undermines trust within the community and harms social relationships. In the *Pistic* (*Faith*) aspect, man would have violated the norms related to faithfulness and ultimate commitments. By committing theft, one betrays personal or communal commitments, affecting the sphere of trust and faith. By now you can see that by violating even one of the commandments, you violate the law in many ways and at various points. Perhaps this is what Van Til was getting at when he wrote:

> But when man broke the law at one point he broke it at every point. The moral and the physical [Creational] are

inextricably interwoven.[3]

Now that we have a rudimentary understanding of "Creational Law" and its distinction from, while at the same time its interwoven nature with, "Scriptural Law", it is necessary that we now turn our attention to "Scriptural Law".

## The Scriptural Law

First of all, what exactly do I mean by the term "Scriptural"? I mean the *inscripturated* revelation of God. As it concerns the Old Testament (though what follows certainly applies to the New), since that is where we find the Ten Commandments first delivered to God's people, we are told that man did not write Scripture merely out of a whim or because he thought it was a good idea. On the contrary, we are told that Scripture came about because God commanded it. From the time of Adam to the time of Moses, the revealed and preached revelation of God had been primarily orally communicated, but the time had come, under the prophet Moses, for the revealed Word to be written, to be *inscripturated*. As the biblical scholar Dr. Joel R. Beeke wrote:

> As Israel traveled from the Red Sea to Mount Sinai, the Lord told Moses, "Write this… in a book" (Ex. 17:14). After God spoke his laws to Moses on the mountain, not only did Moses preach them to the people but also

---

3.  Ibid., 13.

"Moses Breaks the Tables of the Law" (Exod. 32:19) by Gustave Doré, 1866.

wrote "all the words of the LORD" (24:4)... It was God's will that Israel have a written record of his covenant with them (24:7; Deut. 17:18) – the "book of the law." These scrolls contained not only the statutes of the covenant but historical records of Israel's experiences (Ex. 17:14; Num. 33:2).[4]

The inscripturation of the revealed Word of God, therefore, was the *command of God*, not something that originated from the mind of man. The apostle Peter

---

4.   Joel R. Beeke, *Reformed Systematic Theology, Vol. 1: Revelation and God* (Wheaton, IL.: Crossway, 2019), 320.

states this in his second letter in the New Testament, writing: "For no prophecy was ever produced by the will of man, but men spoke from God as they were carried along by the Holy Spirit" (2 Pt. 1:21). However, as it concerns the Ten Commandments, there is one particular detail that sets it apart from the rest of the Scriptural writings. It is still inspired as the rest of the Scriptures, but while the rest of the Scriptures were written by human hands, guided by the Spirit of God, the Ten Commandments were *not* originally written by human hands. On the contrary, they were written by the hand of God. Consider what it says in Exodus 31:18,

> And he gave to Moses, when he had finished speaking with him on Mount Sinai, the two tablets of the testimony, tablets of stone, written with the finger of God.

The fact that the Ten Commandments were written with the "finger of God", to cite the text *precisely*, demonstrates the unique character of the Law. The Ten Commandments were rooted in the nature of God and in the order of God's creation, which reveals the will and character of God. These Ten Commandments, what we might call the "moral law", is distinct from the other laws that would follow suit, which we could call the "civil/judicial" and the "ceremonial". This detail, of the inscripturation of the Law by God's hand and not man's, is remarkable in its own right. And it explains why the Law of God was so highly elevated, so highly respected and reverenced by the people of God, because there was no question that it originated from the *one true God*. As Beeke wrote:

> The Lord wills that the written word rule and direct his people. God expected Israel to be a literate society (cf. Deut. 24:1, 3) and to publicly display the written words of God in order to shape their domestic and civil life. Leaders were to read it carefully and follow its precepts. Every seven years, the priests were to read the law "before all Israel," including the children, so that the nation would "learn to fear the LORD your God" (31:10-13). God made his covenant people a people of the Book, and he defined their reverential worship with him by the written words of his prophets (28:58).[5]

Now, of course, we are not ignorant of the many arguments laid against the credibility of how these Ten Commandments came to be. One popular argument has to do with the Code of Hammurabi,[6] which were Babylonian laws that supposedly originated, according to the ancient Babylonians, from the Babylonian god Marduk, who gave it, inscribed in stone, to King Hammurabi (ca. 1728-1686 BC). The argument is that the Jews adopted and edited the Code of Hammurabi, and invented the story of how the Ten Commandments came to be, extracting as inspiration the ancient Bab-

5.   Ibid., 320.

6.   See "The Code of Hammurabi, translated by L. W. King", *The Avalon Project (Yale Law School)*. Accessed May 14, 2024, https://avalon.law.yale.edu/ancient/hamframe.asp/.

*Détail de la stèle du Code de Hammurabi, roi de Babylone (musée du Louvre)*, CC BY-SA 3.0.

ylonian account. Of course, some have played mathematical/historical gymnastics trying to place the Ten Commandments prior to the Code of Hammurabi, but the fact that the Code of Hammurabi came to be first (1755–1750 BC) is not reason for us to consider the argument made against the Ten Commandments as valid. There are two matters that can be addressed in this common argument, the first is that the concept of law is not something exclusively unique to the people of God. We live in a world of laws, and because we live in such a world, we cannot help but presuppose law. However, the natural man, corrupted by his sinfulness, cannot help but distort the true law and fashion it into something of his own making. Where did this true law come from if the Ten Commandments had not yet been given? Well, the true law was inscribed originally in the hearts of men. Having been created in the image of God, man was originally righteous, he reflected the perfect righteousness of God prior to the fall. When man fell into sin, the divine image he bore was not erased, it was marred, and for this reason man knows that there is a law, a true law, but having had his divine image marred, and having fallen from the glory of God, he cannot help but distort the law into something of his own making. We should not, therefore, be surprised by the early date of the Code of Hammurabi, it simply affirms the biblical truth that mankind was created in the image of God, and that there still lies vestiges of his original righteousness, though they are overshadowed by the pervasive and corruptive influence of his sin.

The second matter is that we should not be surprised that the Babylonians came up with this idea of Marduk giving the transcribed law unto King Hammurabi. If the King wanted to establish an ideal society, which was his plan, and to eradicate wickedness, though he was ignorant to the fact that he too was wicked, he had to have a law that was worthy enough in its own right to be respected by all people. And how else to accomplish this than to say that the law originated from their chief deity? Hammurabi was on to something, a law that originates from the divine is a law that demands respect, it carries authoritative weight, but unfortunately for Hammurabi, his law was just as much a work of his own doing as the god Marduk was the work of his—and the Babylonian's—imagination. The Ten Commandments, in contrast, was the true law, undefiled, written by the finger of God, and given unto man. I should add, it was written *twice* by the finger of God. It had to be done a second time because on the first occasion, Moses broke the tablets in anger after seeing Israel engaged in the worship of a golden calf (Exod. 31:18; 32:19). Now, God did not permit Moses to transcribe it by hand after the first tablets were broken, instead, God gave him a second set of tablets, inscribed by His finger (Exod. 34:1), and it would then be transcribed by Moses in the book of the law and by later scribes. It had to be clear to the people that the Law did not originate from Moses or some created being, *it originated from God Himself.* And this divine inscription foreshadowed that God would again inscribe the law of God, undefiled, in the hearts of men. As the prophet Jeremiah prophesied:

> For this is the covenant that I will make with the house of Israel after those days, declares the LORD: I will put my law within them, and I will write it on their hearts. And I will be their God, and they shall be my people (Jer. 31:33).

To what was God pointing? He was pointing to the coming of the Christ, who would not only fulfill the Law in His earthly ministry, but make it possible for our hearts, by the power of the Spirit of God, to be made *new*, with an inclination, or orientation, toward *loving* and *delighting* in His law (Ps. 1:1-2; 119:97; Jn. 14:21), instead of our fallen disposition of setting ourselves in opposition against it (Ps. 52:3; Rom. 8:7). What was marred by the sin of the first Adam, that being our divine image (Gen. 1:26-27), in other words, would be restored in Christ, the last Adam (1 Cor. 15:45-58).

Of course, the question does arise as to whether the Law still applies today, whether Christ abrogated the Law, or set forth a new law, the "Law of Christ" as some theologians have called it. That is a question I will reserve for the end of our time together, but I will mention that I have written a whole chapter on this matter in my book *Apologetics*, and you would do well to consult that chapter. And what I intend to share with you later today is but a snippet of what is contained within the Foreword I wrote in our textbook for today's seminar, *The Ten Commandments* by Cornelius Van Til.

Before we can discuss the validity and relevance of the Law, I would like for us to first consider the content of the moral law, the Ten Commandments. This will make its relevance all the clearer for us before I even begin to address the question of its present validity.

## The First Table of the Law

We begin by first developing an understanding that the Ten Commandments can be divided into two tables: the first table of the Law, and the second table of the Law. The first table consists of the first commandment down to the fourth commandment, four commandments in total, while the second table consists of the fifth down to the tenth commandment. The first table of the Law addresses man's relationship with God, and the second table of the Law addresses man's relationship with fellow man. Here are the Ten Commandments as laid out in Deuteronomy 5:6-21:

> [6] "'I am the LORD your God, who brought you out of the land of Egypt, out of the house of slavery.
>
> [7] "'You shall have no other gods before me.
>
> [8] "'You shall not make for yourself a carved image, or any likeness of anything that is in heaven above, or that is on the earth beneath, or that is in the water under the earth. [9] You shall not bow down to them or serve them; for I the LORD your God am a jealous God, visiting the iniquity of the fathers on the children to the third and fourth generation of those who hate me, [10] but showing steadfast love to thousands of those who love me and keep my commandments.
>
> [11] "'You shall not take the name of the LORD your God in vain, for the LORD will not hold him guiltless who takes his name in vain.
>
> [12] "'Observe the Sabbath day, to keep it holy, as

the LORD your God commanded you. ¹³ Six days you
shall labor and do all your work, ¹⁴ but the seventh day
is a Sabbath to the LORD your God. On it you shall
not do any work, you or your son or your daughter or
your male servant or your female servant, or your ox or
your donkey or any of your livestock, or the sojourner
who is within your gates, that your male servant and
your female servant may rest as well as you. ¹⁵ You
shall remember that you were a slave in the land of
Egypt, and the LORD your God brought you out from
there with a mighty hand and an outstretched arm.
Therefore the LORD your God commanded you to
keep the Sabbath day.

¹⁶ "'Honor your father and your mother, as
the LORD your God commanded you, that your days
may be long, and that it may go well with you in the
land that the LORD your God is giving you.

¹⁷ "'You shall not murder.

¹⁸ "'And you shall not commit adultery.

¹⁹ "'And you shall not steal.

²⁰ "'And you shall not bear false witness against your
neighbor.

²¹ "'And you shall not covet your neighbor's wife. And
you shall not desire your neighbor's house, his field, or
his male servant, or his female servant, his ox, or his
donkey, or anything that is your neighbor's.'"

This text in Deuteronomy, what we might call "The
Decalogue", is the second time that the Ten Com-

This fragment from the Dead Sea scrolls, 4Q41, has been named the "Ten Commandments scroll" because it preserves the entire Decalogue, the Ten Commandments.

mandments are presented, the first time is in Exodus 20:1-17. In the instance of the Exodus text, the Ten Commandments were given in light of the covenant that God was making with His people shortly after they were liberated from Egypt, this event took place on Mount Sinai. While it is true that the Law was specifically given to Israel, it was meant for all humanity, because Israel was to demonstrate to the world, as a beacon in the darkness, how man *ought to live* in relation to God and in relation to fellow man. In the instance of the Deuteronomy text, Moses recites the Ten Commandments as they prepare to enter the Promised Land, this takes place about 40 years *after* the events at Sinai. If you are familiar with the story of the Exodus, you will know that the Israelites were subjected to 40 years of wandering in the wilderness because they were a rebellious people. They doubted that God would fulfill His promise after having witnessed the power of His hand in bringing them out of Egypt and destroying the armies of Pharoah, the latter shortly after having split the Red Sea so that they could cross (Exod. 14-15). The Exodus narrative is filled with wonder and the awe-inspiring power of God. When the time had come for God's people to send spies into the land of Canaan, the Promised Land, they sent twelve spies, and out of the twelve only two gave a positive account (Num. 13). The other ten spies made it seem impossible that God would fulfill His promise, and as a result of the rebellion that arose shortly thereafter (Num. 14), God declared that the generation that left Egypt would die in the wilderness (Deut. 1:35), while the generation that followed would enter the Promised Land—and enter they did, under the leadership of Joshua (Josh. 1). What is worth mentioning, because we see also the faithfulness of God in this instance (as we do in all of Scripture), Caleb in his old age, who was one of the original twelve spies who went into the land and returned to give a positive report, was permitted to enter the Promised Land because of his steadfast faith in the Lord. And old man Caleb did not sit on the sidelines when they entered the Promised Land! He engaged in battle against the Lord's enemies (Num. 14:6-9; Josh. 14).

Returning now to the content of the Ten Commandments, and having understood how it can be divided into *two* tables of the Law, we begin with the first table of the Law, with the first of the four commandments.

## The First Commandment

This is the first commandment, Deuteronomy 5:6-7,

"'I am the Lord your God, who brought you out of the land of Egypt, out of the house of slavery. You shall have no other gods before me." The principle of the first commandment is given to us in the *Shema Israel* in Deuteronomy 6:4-5, which reads: "Hear, O Israel: The LORD our God, the LORD is one. You shall love the LORD your God with all your heart and with all your soul and with all your might." These two verses are what is recited by the Jews as their morning and evening prayers, and they were considered by the Rabbis to not only express the *principle* of the first commandment, or even the first table of the Law, but "to contain the principles of the Decalogue",[7] and this is in fact what Jesus taught in Matthew 22:35-40: that the whole Law can be summed up in two commands, the first, the *Shema Israel*, and the second, to love one's neighbour as oneself. It could therefore be said that the *Shema Israel* does not exclusively express the first commandment but *all the ten commandments*.

Now, in this declaration of the first commandment, God identifies Himself as the self-sufficient, absolute Being. There is no other absolute. If you recall the fifteen aspects of "Creational Law", from the arithmetical, to the biotic, to the pistical (faith), etc., well, sinful man always tends to absolutize some aspect of the creational aspect (or modal) scale. The absolutization of some aspect of creation, of some created thing

---

7.    Rabbi Dr. I Epstein, ed., *The Babylonian Talmud, Seder Nezikin*, vol. IV, *Aboth* (London: The Soncino Press, 1935), 22, n. 8.

or ideal, is the inevitable result of man's denial of God. In order to live and breathe in this world, in order to *function* as a living being, we need an absolute. And by denying God as the self-sufficient absolute, the One in whom all things hold together, the One in whom all things find their meaning, sinful man cannot help but prop up some absolute in God's place. Sigmund Freud had the psychical (psychology) as his absolute (we might even add the sexual, if you are familiar with his perverted psychological theories); Karl Marx had the economical as his absolute; Charles Darwin had the biotic (evolutionism) as his absolute; Stephen Hawking had the physical (the laws of physics) as his absolute— for some of you, this is a review of what we had covered in our last seminar. Well, God makes clear that *He* is the absolute. And in this declaration, He reminds Israel that *He* is their Saviour. So, we have God as absolute, God as Saviour, and that the relationship that He has with His people is *one of grace*. As the biblical scholar R.J. Rushdoony (1916-2001) wrote, "God chose Israel, not Israel God."[8] Furthermore, it is made clear in God's declaration that the Law is *given* to the people of grace, and as I had stated earlier, it is implied that this Law would be held up to the world as the definitive standard by which man ought to live in relation to God and in relation to fellow man. While for those who are perishing the Law is judgment to them, to those who

---

8.  R. J. Rushdoony, *The Institutes of Biblical Law* (Phillipsburg, NJ.: P&R Publishing, 1973), 15.

are called by God's grace, it is understood in the light of God's grace. As Rushdoony writes:

> The law is given to the people saved by grace as their way of grace, to set forth the privilege and blessing of the covenant.[9]

What covenant? The covenant between God and His people. And how should Israel respond to such grace? With the first commandment, "You shall have no other gods before me." No other gods. No polytheism, no henotheism, no pantheism, no -isms, *only monotheism*, the worship of the One true God. So, we see here a positive command and a negative one: The positive command is to worship God, to serve God, in every aspect of life. The negative command is not to worship anything else outside of God, because there is only one God. We could spend hours studying this first commandment alone, but we have another nine to go through, so let me just say this before we move on: This first commandment is the foundation of man's *moral* life, and by *moral*, I mean how man out to live before the face of God. Morality in this fallen world can mean almost anything, it is a malleable concept that has changed over the course of time according to the changing philosophies of fallen man. But "morality" according to God, what it means to be "moral", is very clearly defined, and it is defined by God's Law. It is not malleable and dependent upon the times, but

---

9. Ibid.

rather, unchanging, because God Himself is unchanging. "What then does it mean to be moral?" we might ask. To be *moral* is to live before the face of God in obedience to the Law of God. This is what the Bible identifies as *righteousness*.

## The Second Commandment

What then follows as the second commandment? Deuteronomy 5:8-9b, "You shall not make for yourself a carved image, or any likeness of anything that is in heaven above, or that is on the earth beneath, or that is in the water under the earth. You shall not bow down to them or serve them...." Time does not permit us to examine the rest of verse 9 and verse 10, so we will look at the essence of this second commandment which I have just read. If the first commandment was the foundation to moral living, and this implied serving God alone in every aspect of life, this second commandment can be understood as the foundation and guiding principle for our worship. Van Til put it this way:

> The first commandment teaches us that we must serve God; the second how we can do this correctly as far as the external expression of religion is concerned. Thus these two commandments relate to altogether distinct matters.[10]

What is explicitly stated in this second commandment? That we are not to have images made of God

---

10. Van Til, *The Ten Commandments*, 51.

or of anything in heaven. If you have perhaps noticed by now, the church we are meeting in today does not have a single portrait or statue of Jesus, or of Mary, or of any of the saints or angels. There are two framed facsimile pages of Scripture, one being a portion of the Isaiah scroll from the Dead Sea Scroll collection, and the other a page from *La Biblia del Oso*, which was translated by the Spanish reformer Casiodoro de Reina. None of these two framed facsimiles are second commandment violations. Now, the reason we do not have images, whether painted, or carved, is because these images firstly fall short of God's true glory and image, and second, they are a temptation to man in terms of the object of his worship. Reformed protestant churches are known to not have such images and sculptures. The Roman Catholic church, on the other hand, is littered with images and sculptures, and not just within the churches but also within the homes of their members. These images, otherwise referred to as "icons", are considered mediums through which man can worship God. But they are a blatant violation of the second commandment. Now, you may notice certain Christian publications portraying Jesus in some form of art, whether this be as a portrait, a comic, a painting, etc. Such images of Jesus as a human person are not necessarily violations of the second commandment, because they emphasize Jesus' human nature. They are not being presented as objects of worship, nor as icons through which man can worship God, but rather as a symbolic presentation of Jesus as a human person within the context of our protestant creed and the narrative of Scripture. But let us say that someone decided to draw God, not Jesus in His humanity, but the divine nature of God Himself, whether the Father, the Holy Spirit, or the Holy Trinity, etc., such an image would be a clear second commandment violation. So, we can see, based on how it has been written, just how *specific* this second commandment is, but there is also a general command here and that is to *not* commit idolatry. In other words, "do not worship anything other than God." You can see then what Van Til meant by the interrelationship between this commandment and the first. And to comment on the rest of verse 9 and verse 10, without going into too much depth, consider again the words of Rushdoony:

> ...even as a very literal idolatry is forbidden, so a very literal blessing and curse are attached to the law. This is clearly stated in the declaration of the commandment... A very literal law has very literal and material consequences. Obedience and disobedience have central historical consequences and results.[11]

While Rushdoony speaks *contextually* about the nation of Israel here, he also means this *generally* in relation to people everywhere. Nations who worship God as He deserves to be worshipped, as He commands *how* to be worshipped, will be blessed, whereas those na-

---

11. Rushdoony, *The Institutes of Biblical Law*, 21.

tions who have fallen to idolatry will suffer historical consequences and results. I dread to even consider the consequences that are yet to come upon our country Canada, which has strayed so far from its early Christian consensus and convictions. The commandment is clear, "do not worship idols"—violate this command and there will be consequences subject to the sovereignty and providence of God; fulfill this command, and thus worship God alone, and there will be blessing. Israel would taste both the blessing and the consequences throughout their history according to how they lived in relation to God, with Whom they had a covenant.

## The Third Commandment

What now follows as the third commandment? Deuteronomy 5:11, "'You shall not take the name of the Lord your God in vain, for the Lord will not hold him guiltless who takes his name in vain....'" You are all perhaps aware just how widespread profanity has become in our culture. Whether it is hearing someone curse on a bus, or in a park, or on the street, or on the radio and media. It has grown exponentially since generations past. Cindy and I used to watch the latest movies that came out, we were *cinephiles*, but the more we watched what was pumped out of Hollywood, the more we noticed just how much heavier the profanity became, and not just general profanity, but particularly the use of the Lord's name in vain. The term "for God's sake" is one

*Baroque painting of the death of Uzzah (1704)* by Giulio Quaglio the Younger
in Ljubljana Cathedral.

such manner of using the Lord's name in vain, but because that was not enough, we now have the term "for
Christ's sake", and if that is not enough, then they add
an expletive with the phrase. And that is just scratching
the surface. Sinful man cannot help but express such
hostility because the sin in his heart reigns supreme,
and it appears that he is just never content with how
much he drags God's name in the mud. You know, I
say "mud", but mud itself is not unclean. When Uzzah,
during the reign of King David, attempted to prevent
the ark of the covenant from falling off the cart and on

to the mud, what did God say when he touched the ark? Did God say, "Thank you Uzzah! You kept my ark clean!" No, God said no such thing. Instead, Uzzah was struck down by God (1 Chron. 13:10). Do you know why? Because Uzzah assumed that his hands were cleaner than the mud. What is mud but God's creation? The mud did not do *anything* to desecrate its Creator. Man, on the other, committed treason against God by means of his sin, by violating God's Law. Uzzah may have meant well, but his hands were dirtied by his sin. The profane cannot have fellowship with the sacred. Man, therefore, does not drag God's name through the mud, as the saying usually goes, he drags God's name through his sin. Now, surely Israel would not have steeped so low, but while they may not have violated this third command as flagrantly as we do in our culture today, they did violate this command by swearing false oaths with God's name. To make an oath, to swear to do something in the name of the Lord, meant that you would keep your word as God Himself is faithful. And to make such an oath was necessary at times because in a fallen world, man's word alone cannot be trusted. To make an oath with the Lord's name meant that if the oath were broken, God's judgment could fall upon the oath-breaker, but swearing by God's name, if done right, also testified of God's faithfulness, and this in turn glorified God. However, to make an oath, knowing that you could not or would likely not keep your word, was to use the name of the Lord in vain.

God is holy, faithful, and true, and He will not allow anyone to slander His name. God is not a liar, God is not unfaithful, and God will call every vain word to account (Matt. 12:36).

## The Fourth Commandment

What now is the fourth commandment? Let us look at Deuteronomy 5:12-14, "Observe the Sabbath day, to keep it holy, as the Lord your God commanded you. Six days you shall labor and do all your work, but the seventh day is a Sabbath to the Lord your God." This fourth commandment is one which we can identify as a *creation ordinance*, that is to say, it is rooted in the created order of God by nature of the fact that, after having created the cosmos in six days, God took the seventh day to rest. God did not rest because He was tired, instead, He took the day to rest because His creative work had finished, and He intended to model to man that, within the context of his work, rest would be necessary. Man, therefore, was to follow suit and rest on the seventh day from all his labour. While it is true that the Jewish Sabbath (*Shabbat*) is not imposed upon us today, the Law-principle of the Sabbath has carried down to us in the context of the new covenant in Jesus Christ. In the Old Testament, man was to keep the Sabbath holy, that is to say, he was to rest from his labour *in order to spend the day meditating upon God and His goodness*. We could say that it was a day to delight in the Lord and in His precepts. But there was also a theological significance attached to the Sabbath. Because the Lord knew, in His omniscience, that man would fall into sin, He placed the Sabbath at the end of the week knowing of the anticipatory hope that man would have for the rest he would find in his redemption. In other words, being at the end of the week, man would look forward to his day of rest, in the same way, man would look forward to the day that the promised seed comes, for in that day, he will find rest for his weary soul. What was it that Jesus said to those who were tired and weary? "Come to me, all who labor and are heavy laden, and I will give you rest" (Matt. 11:28). With the first advent of the Christ, the Sabbath changes. When does it change? Not during Jesus' earthly ministry, but after His resurrection. We no longer refer to the Sabbath as the Sabbath, but rather, we refer to it as "The Lord's Day." And when is the Lord's Day? At the beginning of the week, the Sunday. Why was there this change of day? Because we no longer have an anticipatory hope for the *first* coming of the promised seed, He has already come. We certainly have an anticipatory hope for the *second* coming of the Lord, but we do not have to wait until the second coming in order to receive and experience the rest that Jesus promised His people. We now look back instead toward the first day of the week because it was a Sunday that Jesus rose from the dead, hence why it is called "The Lord's Day." We look *back* in memory of what Jesus secured for us, His people. And what did He secure for us exactly? Consider the first paragraph of the eighth chapter of the 1689 London Baptist Confession of Faith, it reads:

> It pleased God, in His eternal purpose, to choose and ordain the Lord Jesus, His only begotten Son, according to the covenant made between them both, to be the mediator between God and man; the prophet, priest, and king; head and savior of the church, the heir of all things, and judge of the world; unto whom He did from all eternity give a people to be His seed and to be by Him in time *redeemed, called, justified, sanctified, and glorified.*[12]

The Law-principle of the Sabbath, therefore, has been passed down to us Christians in the form of "The Lord's Day", the Sunday, during which we gather with the saints to worship our Lord, and during which we delight in the Lord as we rest in Him. Should we then abide by this Law-principle? Yes, we absolutely should, because man was created in God's image, and man, as a creature, must image His Creator as much as he possibly can. Can he do this apart from Christ? Absolutely not. Only those who believe, only those who are of God's people, can abide by this Law-principle, because the rest that Christ secured is only for those who call Him Lord. As Van Til writes,

---

12. "Of Christ the Mediator", *The 1689 Baptist Confession of Faith*. Accessed May 17, 2024, https://www.the1689confession.com/1689/chapter-8/, emphasis mine.

In order that man shall truly imitate God, he must be in living contact with God. Thus the sinner must reflectively turn to Paradise past and proleptically to Paradise regained in order to see how the Sabbath should be celebrated. And this the sinner can and will do only if he is connected with Christ. Hence the Sabbath is also called a sign between Yahweh and His people.[13]

## The Second Table of the Law

Having now surveyed the first table of the Law, you can tell by now that not only does the first table address man's relationship to God, it also reveals *who God is*. He is the only self-sufficient absolute. He is the Saviour of those whom He has called by His grace. He is so glorious and so wonderful and so transcendent that to be likened to carved images or sculptures would be flagrantly blasphemous, and, therefore, He is to be worshipped according to what He has revealed in order that we might not dishonour Him. What else did we learn from the first table of the Law? That God is holy and worthy of our reverence, truthful in all His ways, faithful and unchanging, and that we should never, therefore, use the Lord's name in vain, for when we do, we blaspheme His name and we shall be held to account. We also see, as with the fourth commandment, that God is merciful and gracious. He is not a harsh taskmaster, but rather, arranges a day during the week for man to rest and to become re-centered in the Lord in Whom all things find their meaning. All of life is

---

13. Van Til, *The Ten Commandments*, 104-105.

to be understood in reference to Him, and the fourth commandment allows us to recalibrate our hearts in order that all of life lived may be in reference to God our Creator and Saviour.

What now to say about the second table of the Law? Well, as I had stated, the first table of the Law addresses man's relationship with God. The second table of the Law, however, addresses man's relationship with fellow man. And while there does exist this distinction, the second table of the Law still addresses man's living before the presence of God, before the *face* of God. And how man lives before the face of God either glorifies God or dishonours Him.

## The Fifth Commandment

Let us then continue our survey of the Law with the fifth commandment, the first command of the second table of the Law. Deuteronomy 5:16, "Honor your father and your mother, as the LORD your God commanded you, that your days may be long, and that it may go well with you in the land that the LORD your God is giving you." This fifth commandment is considered the first with a promise, which Paul identifies in Ephesians 6:1-3,

> Children, obey your parents in the Lord, for this is right. "Honor your father and mother" (this is the first commandment with a promise), "that it may go well with you and that you may live long in the land."

This fifth commandment has to do with authority, the authority which God has established on earth, and if we understand authority *biblically*, we know that no authority can be exercised unless it has been given by the Lord. Jesus Himself made this clear when He was interrogated by Pilate, that the only authority Pilate had over Jesus was the authority that the Father had given him for the fulfillment of God's will (Jn. 19:11).

While the fifth commandment does address authority *generally*, it addresses *specifically* the parent-child relationship. The father and mother are the authority over their children, with the father serving as the head, and the mother as her husband's support. As you well know, fathers are not always home throughout the week, they carry most of the weight to support the home, and I say "most" because, in an ideal world, this would only be the man's responsibility, but given our ailing economy, mothers are often in need of entering the labour force. But it was always intended, according to the created order that God had established in the creation of Adam and Eve, that the husband go out into the world to work, and that the wife tend to her husband, which included caring for and raising his children. The father, however, though he may be absent due to work, was not to be absent in the raising of his children. His work, in other words, is not to be considered as an excuse to remove himself from the child-rearing process. The father, according to God's design, is to exercise his role as head of the family, and therefore, when the father is absent, the wife is to uphold her husband's authority and ensure that their children are made subject to their joint authority. Therefore, since God had placed father and mother—and note that the Bible is very clear here in identifying father and mother, not person and person, or father and father, or mother and mother, but one biological male and one biological woman—the child is to honour the authority that God has placed over him. And I say "authority" in the *singular* and not the plural because, although father and mother are two distinct persons, being joined together in marriage (and marriage *biblically* defined), they are one flesh and therefore one authority over their children. If children then obey their parents, if they obey their father and mother, and so long as this obedience does not conflict with the revealed truth of God and how we ought to live before Him, then they will be blessed by God. But if they do not honour their parents, then no assurance is given that their life will go well, because by refusing to acknowledge and submit to the authority that God has established over them, they will also then be refusing to submit to the authority of God, who is sovereign and absolute. Did not Paul say that we should submit and pray for the civil authorities placed over us? Because it is God who places authorities over us.

As much as I would love to, I am afraid that I will not be able to go into the specifics of civil disobedience and when it is biblically justified, such a discussion certainly finds its place under the fifth commandment, but what I will simply say is that an excellent book that touches on the subject is Francis Schaeffer's (1912-1984) *A Christian Manifesto*, which not only identifies the limits of civil obedience, but the use of civil disobedience and the use of force. Consider Schaeffer's work then as additional reading to supplement the textbook which you have been provided with today.

## The Sixth Commandment

We have to keep the ball rolling here. So, we now have the sixth commandment, "You shall not murder." While it is true that man should not indiscriminately kill every plant and animal, and that we should be careful stewards of God's creation, we do recognize that in this fallen world, these plants and animals are meant to be for man's use and that taking their life is necessary (e.g., food). However, this sixth commandment addresses man taking the life of another. In its positive form, this commandment means that we are to protect and preserve human life, that we are to seek the flourishing of the life of our neighbour. And in its negative form, this commandment means that we are not to take a life. One might ask about the death penalty which was instituted by the Law of Moses, but the death penalty had to be understood within the context of the Law, the Mosaic juridical system, and that this commandment concerned man arbitrarily, or for any other reason outside of the Law, taking another man's life. If a man, amongst the Israelites, did murder another man, what was the consequence? Death. Why death? Because the severity of the penalties prescribed in the Mosaic Law were tied to the value and significance of what the Law sought to protect. And the life of man is of great value, why? Because man bears God's image. As a matter of fact, it is because we bear God's image that we have such a concept such as "human dignity", and unbelievers can never take that away from us.[14] As Van Til wrote,

> It is often admitted, even by those averse to the creation doctrine, that Christianity has introduced the idea of the inherent value of human personality. Now, in so far as it is true that Christians stands for the value of personality as such, it has not introduced it but *reintroduced* it.[15]

## The Seventh Commandment

Thus far we have seen how the fifth commandment seeks to protect the authority which God has placed within the family, how the sixth commandment seeks to protect human life, and now in the seventh commandment we see how it seeks to protect the created order of marriage. When God created Adam and Eve, not only as male and female, but as husband and wife, He created them as the paradigm for all marriages

---

14. See Michael Nazir-Ali, *The Unique and Universal Christ: Jesus in a Plural World* (Colorado Springs, CO.: Paternoster, 2008).

15. Van Til, *The Ten Commandments*, 133.

to come. In what sense? That marriage would be between one man and one woman. Consider Genesis 2:24, "Therefore a man shall leave his father and his mother and hold fast to his wife, and they shall become one flesh." And this husband and wife, according to Paul, manifests in their marriage the mystery of God in relation to Christ and the church. A married couple, in other words, are to reflect unto the world what the relationship between Christ and the church is. What might be an example? When one sins against another, and repentance follows, the one who forgives reflects the grace that God extends to the church for its sins. And when the wife submits to the husband, she reflects the submission of the church to its head, who is Christ. And when the husband treats his wife well, and goes even as far as to sacrifice himself for her wellbeing, he reflects the love and care that Christ has for His church, which brought Christ to the point of death on a cross (Eph. 5:25-33). Of course, when husband and wife do not model who Christ is, and instead decide to model dishonesty, betrayal, unfaithfulness, and abuse, then they profane God's name and blaspheme the image of Christ by portraying a false image of who He is, how He is with His people, and how His people ought to be with Him. Marriage is truthfully a beautiful institution ordained by God, it is a creation ordinance, and as such, it needs to be protected. Nowadays, marriage has been re-defined, and to not comply with this re-definition means to be politically incorrect and non-inclusive, and while we are to be gentle and sensitive to those whom we disagree with, we are not to compromise on what God has established in His Word, especially in light of the fact that all things are to be understood in reference to Him. In other words, marriage is to be understood in reference to God, and in reference to God we understand marriage to be as between one man and one wife. All deviations from this are sinful. This includes taking more than one wife. This includes amassing for oneself concubines. And for our contemporary application (it was certainly applicational back then too), this includes committing adultery. Man was not to violate the marriage of another, or his own marriage for that matter. Marriage, as defined by God, as instituted by God, was so precious, so sacred, that adultery under the Mosaic Law was punishable by death (Lev. 20:10). Do not misunderstand me, I am not saying that the capital punishment should be reinstituted for cases of adultery, but do not lose sight of what the severity of the punishment says about the value of marriage. While the juridical penalties of the Law, as they were carried out by Old Testament Israel, have not been passed down to us, the Law in principle still remains. In the positive form, we are to protect and preserve marriage. And in the negative form, we are not to violate the marriage covenant of another by committing adultery.

Fidel Castro and Camilo Cienfuegos entering Havana after the rebel victory, 8 January 1959. Cuba is a modern-day example of the failures of Marxist economic theories and models.

## The Eighth Commandment

That now brings me to the eighth commandment, Deuteronomy 5:19, "And you shall not steal." What does this commandment seek to protect? It seeks to protect man's right to private property. Marxists have claimed that the problem of man and of all his societal ills is due to *capital*, and hence capitalism. Read his Karl Marx's book *Das Kapital* (1867). The right to private property is seen, from his eyes, as an evil. And so, what have Marxist governments done? Look at what the Soviet Union did. Look at what Cuba did. They wanted to be rid of the right to private property, so the state took all the property and evenly distributed it to all the people, which to put it simply meant that the state became rich and the people became poor! Well, Marx certainly had it wrong. Perhaps you have heard this, but today there are "Christian" Marxists who think that Christ would have been a Marxist if He had come in our time. But—laying aside that blasphemous statement of "Christian" Marxists—as we can see in the Law of God, which *originated* from God, and which *expresses* the will of God, private property is presupposed, and therefore, in a positive form, the right to private property is to be respected, and in a negative form, man is not to steal what belongs to another. We might ask, why is private property necessary at all? Why is part of our created reality? Why cannot we do without it? Van Til explains this better than I:

> Now, since man is created soul and body, he needs an external sphere in which he can act freely. He needs this sphere in connection and conjointly with others since together they form unity, but he also needs a sphere for himself where he can develop himself in relative independence. *Property* gives freedom for rational and moral activity.[16]

## The Ninth Commandment

We need to keep pressing on. The ninth commandment, Deuteronomy 5:20, states: "And you shall not

---

16. Ibid., 168, italicism mine.

bear false witness against your neighbor." What does this commandment address? The truth. In its most simplest form we could say, "Thou shalt not lie", but as with the other commandments, there is a positive form and a negative form, or a positive command and a negative command. The positive is that we are to protect and preserve the truth, at all times. In our last seminar I had talked about how the truth of God—the truth about how all things truly are, not according to us but according to what God has revealed, for He is truth itself—the truth is the *Thesis*. And all that is contrary to the truth is the *Antithesis*. We are, therefore, to communicate the truth concerning all things, in all aspects of life. That means in personal relations, in professional settings, in scientific spheres, in every imaginable context, the truth must reign supreme. And who is the truth? Christ, who said that not only is He the way and the life, but He is also "the truth" (John 14:6). The negative form of this commandment is, therefore, do not lie, do not propagate the lie, do not advance or endorse or entertain that which is contrary to the *Thesis*, to the truth of God, even in the most simplest of conversations with your neighbour. What you say, as a Christian, either reflects the true nature of our God, who is truth, or we profane His name by lying and therefore suggesting, by our behaviour, that God is a liar. Such an offense is not to be considered lightly. Embrace, uphold, and defend the *Thesis*, and reject the *Antithesis*, and any potential for a pagan *Synthesis*.[17]

## The Tenth Commandment

And finally, the tenth commandment, which we find in Deuteronomy 5:21:

> And you shall not covet your neighbor's wife. And you shall not desire your neighbor's house, his field, or his male servant, or his female servant, his ox, or his donkey, or anything that is your neighbor's.

What does this commandment address? It addresses desire. In one of our past studies on the 1689 London Baptist Confession, we had occasion to touch on desire in relation to temptation and sin. I will summarize that for you here: When we are tempted, we have not erred against the Lord, even if the temptation is aimed toward some area of personal vulnerability. But the moment that we *desire* whatever we are tempted with, the moment we *entertain* the temptation, we have already sinned. And if we do not address that sin in our hearts, if we do not put a stop to it and repent of it, if we do not kill sin, then that desire will give birth to the works of the flesh, and that will in turn produce death. In one of his sermons, Dr. Beeke touched on this matter of desire and its association with sin. He said:

> John Owen [the puritan] said so famously, "Be killing sin, or sin will be killing you." "Be killing sin, or sin will

---

17. See H. Evan Runner, *Point Counter Point: Paideia Monographs* (Jordan Station, ON.: Paideia Press, 2020).

be killing you." You see, to kill sin, to clear the woods of sin in our heart, is a critical part of the whole process of sanctification. And the more we experience that, the more assurance we will have that our desires are God-ward and therefore that we are the children of God.[18]

Just to be clear, "desire" itself is not sinful, because we can desire that which is holy, righteous, and pure, but desire, like any other expression that springs forth from our hearts, can be tainted by sin. And a heart poisoned with sin will give expression to sinful desire. What then is the positive form of this command? That we seek to protect and preserve godly desire. And the negative form? That we do not desire that which is sinful.

## The Relevance of the Law

Now, what I had earlier promised: Is the Law still valid and relevant today? And by the Law, I mean the Ten Commandments. The matter of the civil/juridical and the ceremonial is for another day. The answer is yes to both. I think the relevance of the Law has already been understood as we surveyed the commandments, but what about its validity? The affirmative answer concerning its validity should not be taken on my own authority, but on the authority of Jesus. In His Sermon on the Mount, Matthew 5:17, Jesus states: "Do not think that I have come to abolish the Law or the

18. Joel Beeke, "Be Killing Sin, Or Sin Will Be Killing You", *Ligonier*. Accessed May 17, 2024, https://www.ligonier.org/posts/be-killing-sin-or-sin-will-be-killing-you/.

Prophets; I have not come to abolish them but to fulfill them." Jesus clearly says that He had not come to abolish the Law, and therefore, we are not to conclude that Jesus came to give us a "new" Law. No, Jesus affirmed the Law, and then He elevated the Law to a higher spiritual plane. To look at a person lustfully is to commit adultery within our own hearts. To hate a person without cause is to commit murder within our own hearts. Etc. (Matt. 5:21-22; 27-28). And in the few verses that follow, Jesus explains that he who obeys and teaches the Law shall be considered great in the kingdom of heaven, while those who give the least importance to even the smallest aspect of the Law shall be considered least in the kingdom of heaven (Matt. 5:18-19). Jesus did not come to abolish the Law, He came to re-issue it as part of His inauguration message for the kingdom that He had come to establish. Jesus, the King, the Ruler of the kingdom of God, *delighted* in the Law, because He *gave* it, and we too are to delight in it. When relating the Law to Christ and God's grace and the role it plays for us today, Rushdoony has this to say:

> The expression, "dead to the law," is indeed in Scripture (Gal. 2:9; Rom. 7:4), but it has reference to the believer in relationship to the atoning work of Christ as the believer's representative and substitute; the believer is dead to the law as an indictment, a legal sentence of death against him, Christ having died for him, but the believer is alive to the law as the righteousness of God. The purpose of Christ's atoning work was to

restore man to a positive of covenant-keeping instead of covenant-breaking, to enable man to keep the law by freeing man "from the law of sin and death" (Rom. 8:2), "that the righteousness of the law might be fulfilled in us" (Rom. 8:4). Man is restored to a position of law-keeping. The law thus has a position of centrality in man's indictment (as a sentence of death against man the sinner), in man's redemption (in that Christ died, Who although the perfect law-keeper as the new Adam, died as man's substitute), and in man's sanctification (in that man grows in grace as he grows in law-keeping, for the law is the way of sanctification).[19]

Our justification in Christ, therefore, is to be understood as *by the grace of God*; our sanctification, however, is to be understood *by the means of the Law of God*. No doubt, a discussion for another day, as our time has now come to an end. I leave you then with these last words, the words of the Psalmist:

> Blessed is the man
>   who walks not in the counsel of the wicked,
> nor stands in the way of sinners,
>   nor sits in the seat of scoffers;
> but his delight is in the law of the Lord,
>   and on his law he meditates day and night.
> He is like a tree
>   planted by streams of water
> that yields its fruit in its season,
>   and its leaf does not wither.
> In all that he does, he prospers (Ps. 1:1-3).

---

19. Rushdoony, *The Institutes of Biblical Law*, 3.

VIII

# THE WEST AND ITS DON QUIXOTIC SYNDROME

**Date:** June 15, 2024

**Context:** Apologia 2024 Conference

**Setting:** Iglesia Bautista Emanuel, Toronto, Ontario, Canada

### Introductory Remarks

THIS CONFERENCE was put together in collaboration with the Spanish-speaking churches of the Canadian National Baptist Convention (CNBC). It has been our intention, in light of the significant growth in missions work as a convention, that we also provide theologically rich material for the growth and health of the collective church. The church's missiology, after all, cannot go unaccompanied by doctrinal precision. The two must

271

go hand-in-hand, for otherwise, how could we possibly bear witness of a Christian world-and-life view? It is for that reason that we are gathered here today for our Apologia 2024 conference. And it is our hope that this can be one of many conferences where we can address matters that require the utmost attention of the church, particularly as it relates to our witness and our commitment to developing and teaching a distinctly biblical worldview.

*Apologia*, as some of you may know, is a Greek word for a rational "defense", and we most often associate its use and meaning with the passage of 1 Peter 3:15, from which the apologetic discipline first sprang with Scriptural clarity. As a result, this conference is very much *apologetic* in nature, that is to say, it concerns both the defense and the advancement of our Christian worldview. And what most urgent topic to address first, given our cultural conditions and the fact that this is our first apologetic conference together, than the topic of human sexuality and identity?

As you all may well know, June is the month of "Pride" right across Canada, it is what you might call the "holy month" of our nation's pagan religion. And we are right in the middle of it. One might be tempted to think that such a pagan celebration would have no effect on the church so long as the church steps onto the sidelines and minds its own business—and that to address the matter directly would simply accomplish what unbelievers have hoped for, which is to call more

attention to their cause, that being, their fight for freedom. Though, if we were to define what that "freedom"
is, we would simply define it as "freedom from God's
creational norms and law." In other words, what the late
Christian thinker Greg L. Bahnsen (1948-1995) called
*radical autonomy*. And to cite Bahnsen, he means:

> ...being a law unto oneself, so that one's thinking is
> independent of any outside authority, including God's.
> Autonomous reasoning takes itself philosophically as
> the final point of reference and interpretation, the ul-
> timate court of intellectual appeal; it presumes to be
> self-governing, self-determinative, and self-directing.[1]

Well, allowing fallen man to strut his radical autonomy without any opposition, and electing to stand
by the sidelines while our culture becomes further depraved, have not done the Canadian church any good.
And it is much the same South of the border. And what
can be said of what awaits churches in Latin America?
Speaking as one who has been born and raised here, the
ideology of the LGBTQ movement has gradually, over
the course of time, infected not only public national
opinion, but a great number of churches—and while
one might signal the fact that such churches were not
as biblically rooted as they should have been, another
factor to consider is that silence on this matter has led
to increased vulnerability and susceptibility. What do

---

1. Greg L. Bahnsen, *Van Til's Apologetic: Readings & Analysis*
(Phillipsburg, NJ.: P&R Publishing, 1998), 1.

I mean? Well, the youth of our time, have a range of diverse questions regarding what takes place in our culture, what their feelings might be, what they might be wrestling with; and what they have found is that there is no firm counsel in the church, because the church has decided to remain silent on the matter. Well, where do you think our youth will find the answers to their questions if the church remains silent? The world certainly has no shortage of answers, they are most certainly the *wrong* answers, but they are answers, nonetheless. And then we ask ourselves, perhaps with utter despair, as to why our youth have been carried away into Babylon? I think you get the picture, and this has been going on over the past couple of generations in the Canadian landscape. Well, if you are not convinced that the church has been so reluctant to address this matter, and that contrary to my claim, it does indeed care about the threat this poses to the church, as well as the opportunity it provides to proclaim the truth of God, consider just how few are gathered here today. This conference was widely marketed, well beyond our Baptist affiliations, and this conference is smack in the middle of "Pride" month. What other occasion do we need to address this urgent matter? What more needs to happen to realize that this is an urgent matter to discuss? That the apathy of the church is concerning on several fronts? Nonetheless, those of us who are here today will suffice, and I hope—no, I pray—that the church wakes up to its call to be salt and light.

Having now introduced this conference to you, what follows now is a most relevant and important question: Who, or what, is the Cántaro Institute to put together such an apologetic conference to begin with? The Cántaro Institute is a relatively new ministry founded in the year 2020, confessionally reformed, and committed to the advancement of the Christian worldview for the reformation and renewal of the church and culture. Our work as an Institute, as a fellowship of teachers and scholars, consists of *inheriting* our protestant tradition through our research, writing, and lectures—demonstrating the intellectual and lifeful vibrance of the biblical worldview. It also consists of *informing* the church of the relevance and comprehensiveness of the gospel through events, translation and publication of print and web resources. And lastly, of *inspiring* God's people to explore the depths of God's Word and its diverse applications for the reformation and renewal of church and culture.

Now, we are not alone in our efforts today to inform and inspire the church, we are, in fact, accompanied by a most cherished ministry, and by a most dear friend who also serves as an associate of the Institute, Joe Owen, director of *Respuestas en Génesis* (Answers in Genesis, LATAM). He will have his time to speak. My role this morning, however, is to first establish the context, the foundation, upon which we can understand what follows.

Joe (Joseph) Owen of Answers in Genesis speaking at the Apologia 2024 Conference, Toronto, Ontario, one of the specialist itinerant speakers on matters relating to sexuality and gender theory.

## The Development of Western Thought

In order to understand what is taking place today, that is to say, in order to understand our present cultural moment, we need to understand what has brought us here as a people. And by people, I mean, as Western civilization. We are not devoid of a history. We can, in fact, track our history of thought and discern the correlations between the heart commitments of man, his worldview (that is to say, his presuppositions, what he believes to be true), and the various cultural mani-festations over time. I intend to address this in a more general manner, considering that Owen will be addressing this more specifically as it concerns the radical sexual autonomy of man. And to address this in a general sense, I find it helpful to visit *The Roots of Western Culture*, authored by the Dutch philosopher Herman Dooyeweerd (1894-1977), who outlines four basic ground-motives. Those being the Matter-Form scheme of the Greeks, the Grace-Nature scheme of the Scholastics, the Creation-Fall-Redemption scheme of the Reformation, and the Freedom-Nature scheme of the Enlightenment. What is most relevant to our discussion today is the Freedom-Nature scheme or dichotomy, but in order to address that, let me first briefly work our way up from the Greeks.

It is no secret that Greek civilization contributed significantly to the development of Western culture, in fact, it is amongst the Greeks that we first find philosophical thought given expressed form. And what predominantly characterized Greek philosophical thought were the teachings of Plato and Aristotle, who together advocated for a Matter-Form understanding of reality. In other words, they believed reality consisted of two irreconcilable planes. There was the world of Matter, in which we live, and the world of Forms, which is beyond Matter. The world of Matter is but a shadow and imitation of the world of Forms, and no matter how hard one might try, Matter will never be shaped into the perfect Forms. A most common example that is used for this is that of a horse: According to the Greeks, we know what a horse is and what a horse should look like because our souls originally came from the world of Forms, and in the world of Forms there is perfect horse-ness. A skinny horse would therefore prompt us to say that it is not a pure and ideal horse. And the same could be said of trees, frogs, fire, wind, and man, etc. As Dooyeweerd himself articulates, this dualism of Matter-Form manifested in Greek culture and civilization:

> The Greek motive of *matter*, the formless principle of becoming and decay, was oriented to the aspect of movement in temporal reality. It gave Greek thought and all of Greek culture a hint of dark mystery which is foreign to modern thinking. The Greek motive of culture, on the other hand, was oriented to the cultural aspect of temporal reality ("culture" means essentially the free forming of matter). It constantly directed thought to an extrasensory, imperishable *form* of being that transcended the cyclical life stream.[2]

One might ask why the Greeks had developed such a mistaken understanding of reality, but the answer is found in man's fallenness. When man fell into sin, he did not only open the gates to death and destruction, he also brought about a comprehensive fragmentation of his thought, life, and understanding of the world. He looks about at God's creation, sees and knows enough

---

2.    Herman Dooyeweerd, *Roots of Western Culture*, (Jordan Station, ON.: Paideia Press, 2012), 20. Italicism mine.

Parts of Oxyrhynchus Papyri, LII 3679, 3rd century,
containing fragments of Plato's *Republic*.

to be convicted of the truth—for creation is God's general revelation to man—but he suppresses this truth by his sinful nature and exchanges the truth for the lie (Rom. 1:18-25).

After the Greeks, what followed next as the most significant development in Western thought was the birth and growth of the church, and the dialogue that followed between Jerusalem (the Christians) and Athens (the pagans), which eventually gave rise to medieval scholasticism. To put it in brief, the patristics, that is to say, the early church fathers, began to incorporate Greek philosophy into their Christian understanding of the world, believing that such philosophy could be found to be complementary to the revealed truth of Scripture. It was not until Thomas Aquinas that the Grace-Nature scheme, which characterizes much of medieval scholasticism, was firmly cemented.[3] According to this understanding of reality, there was the plane of Grace and the plane of Nature, in which Grace was considered all things sacred, while Nature was considered all things natural, such as the philosophy of the Greeks just as it was in its fallen and pagan form. According to the scholastics, Grace perfected Nature, but the two planes could never be truly reconciled. How could the holy and the just be reconciled with the sinful and the profane? That is not to say that philosophy itself, as a discipline, was sinful or profane, but rather, philosophy based upon anti-biblical presuppositions. Plato was a pagan. Aristotle was a pagan. How could the truth be reconciled with the lie? Either Plato was right about his understanding of the world and God is wrong, or God is right and Plato was wrong—and though we know that God is right, we must also admit that the answer cannot be that *both* are right. If you wonder how the Grace-Nature dualism has influenced the church today, I can point you to the Roman Catholic church which still operates according to Scholastic presuppositional principles, as well as the artificial sacred-secular divide which persists in many protestant

---

3.  See Bernie Van Der Walt, *Thomas Aquinas and the Neo-Thomist Tradition: A Christian-Philosophical Assessment* (Jordan Station, ON.: Paideia Press, 2022).

churches. Namely, that there are certain things deemed "sacred" and other things "secular". But is such a divide a faithful articulation of the true state of things? Of reality? The scholastic certainly thinks so. But then how do we understand the Lordship of Christ over all things? As Dooyeweerd writes:

> Aristotle's Greek view of nature was pagan. Nevertheless, the Roman Catholic ground-motive of nature and grace sought to accommodate the Greek ground-motive to that of divine revelation. The scholastics argued that whatever was subject to birth and death, including human beings, was constituted of matter and form. God created all things according to this arrangement. As a *natural* being, for example, they held that a person consists of a "rational soul" and a "material body." Characterized by its capacity for thought, the rational soul was both the "invisible, essential form" of the body and an imperishable "substance" that could exist apart from the body... But this human "nature," which is guided by the natural light of reason, was not corrupted by sin and thus also does not need to be restored by Christ. Human nature is only "weakened" by the fall. It continues to remain true to its innate "natural law" and possesses an autonomy, a relative independence and self-determination in opposition to the realm of grace of the Christian religion.[4]

To put all this in the vernacular, the fundamental problem of scholasticism was its attempt to harmonize

---

4. Dooyeweerd, *Roots of Western Culture*, 117.

and synthesize Christian theology with the philosophical systems of ancient Greece, leading to a dualistic worldview, where faith and reason were seen as separate realms that needed to be reconciled. What man produced according to his natural reason, as per scholasticism, did not have to be brought subject to the divine revelation of God, nor was it deemed as profane or antithetical, because it was believed that sin merely *weakened* the human person, nothing more. This distorted understanding of reality essentially minimalized the effects of the fall, the scope and severity of sin in the human person, and the now apostate direction of all functions of human life.

Of course, the reformation certainly caught wind of the dangerous implications introduced by scholasticism, and the critique it provided emphasized returning to the authority of Scripture (*Sola Scriptura*) and the sufficiency of faith for understanding God's revelation concerning all things in created reality.[5] This was expressed in the ground-motive of Creation-Fall-Redemption, which upholds that God created all things good, and that His creation reveals God's order and purpose. We can discern order and structure in creation, and an interconnectedness as we consider the various aspects of reality. This ground-motive also upholds what the Scriptures teach concerning the fall of man, in which humanity's disobedience to God led to a fundamental

---

5.   See Chapter 5: The Great Synthesis in Dooyeweerd, *Roots of Western Culture.*

rupture in the created order, introducing sin and bro-
kenness into the world. And unlike the scholastics, this
reformed ground-motive affirms that sin affects every
part of creation, distorting and corrupting it—span-
ning from human relationships to social structures to
even the natural world which is subject to the curse of
the fall. There is certainly no dualism, or irreconcilable
planes of existence in this ground-motive, but we can
say that there is a duality in regards to human nature,
in that human beings are simultaneously bearers of
God's image and fallen creatures. This duality leads to
internal and external conflicts within individuals and
societies, and makes most evident the profound need
for redemption, as we cannot restore our broken relationship with God and the corrupted order of creation
by our own efforts. And finally, the final aspect of the
reformation's ground-motive is redemption. Central to
the biblical narrative is the belief that through Jesus
Christ's life, death, and resurrection, God has initiated
the restoration of fallen creation, and this redemption
is not just about saving individual souls, but about the
renewal of the entire creation. This includes social, cultural, and structural renewal, a progressive restoration
of God's original order and purpose. Every aspect of life
is subject to Christ's redemptive work. There is no sec-
ular-sacred divide. All areas, including politics, science,
art, and daily work are to be transformed by the power
of the gospel.

Unlike the other religious ground-motives which have influenced the development of Western civilization, it is the reformational ground-motive of Creation-Fall-Redemption that gives hope and purpose to human existence. It provides a forward-looking historical perspective, anticipating the ultimate fulfillment of God's redemptive plan.

How does this further contrast from other religious worldviews? Well, the Greek ground-motive led to a devaluation of the material and practical world. The scholastic ground-motive treated the things of God and the things of sinful man as if they were equal and at a level footing, portrayed by its compartmentalized view of life. And the Nature-Freedom ground-motive of the Enlightenment, which we are now about to see, emphasizes the radical autonomy of sinful man, much to his detriment.

This is now the point that I had strived to arrive at, the ground-motive of Nature-Freedom. Finding its roots in the Enlightenment, that rationalist movement of the 18th century, the Nature-Freedom ground-motive turned out to be a fundamental driving force that has significantly shaped Western thought. It was, in many ways, a reaction from the reformed ground-motive as it was man's attempt to do away with God altogether and to assert, once again, his radical autonomy. At a simplistic level, this Nature-Freedom ground-motive essentially embodies a tension between the deterministic view of nature and the ideal of human freedom. There are, in other words, two planes of reality according to this view, and once again, they prove to be irreconcilable. There is the plane of Nature, which is the natural world, and then the plane of human Freedom, which is the radical autonomy of man. Let me try to explain this further: From the plane of Nature, imagine that the world—no, that all of *reality*—is a giant superstructure, a machine, and through scientific endeavours we have sought to understand how it all works, discovering in the process natural laws, or what we could call "creational" laws. Any reasonable Western person would agree with this (though they would prefer to use the term "natural" instead of "creational"). It follows then that if we were to know all the creational laws, and all the starting conditions, then we could predict everything that happens. However, from the plane of Freedom, we come to the understanding that humans are not just machines, we are autonomous in the sense that we can make choices, we have aspirations and dreams, and we can think for ourselves. It follows then that we, as creative and responsible beings,[6] have the freedom to decide what we want to do with our lives. The reason that these two planes prove to be irreconcilable, and therefore untenable as a right understanding of reality, can be discerned by asking a simple question: How can man have true freedom if his world is determined by natural laws? Are not natural laws, or to put

---

6. *Responsible* in the sense that we are responsible for our own actions and decisions, but not ultimately responsible to God.

René Descartes (1596-1650), by Frans Hals, widely considered a
seminal figure in the emergence of modern philosophy and science.
Louvre Museum collection, Richelieu, 2nd floor, room 27. INV. 1317.

it differently, are not God's creational laws, like prison
bars preventing man from fully expressing his desired
freedom as Adam and Eve had sought when they ate
from the forbidden tree? I think you can begin to see
where I am going with this now. You see, if we were to
determine what the underlying ground motive is of our
present culture, we could most certainly say that it is
that of Freedom-Nature, though more so drawn from
Romanticism than Rationalism.

When the Enlightenment gripped the West with
its spirit of scientific empiricism and human reason, it

left man with an emptiness, a void which it could not fill, an inevitable result of denying the transcendental. And so, Romanticism came onto the scene, which was a shift away from the cold rationalism of the Enlightenment and towards, particularly, the emotional and the imaginary. Romanticism is, to this day, remembered as that artistic and intellectual movement of the late 18th century. But it was still undergirded by the Freedom-Nature ground motive. Man still perceived nature as restrictive, as confining, as his "prison cell" so-to-speak, and therefore it was reasoned that man must surpass the boundaries of nature in order to achieve what he so desperately yearns for, *freedom*. The freedom that Adam and Eve sought when they ate from the tree. A freedom to be a law unto themselves. A freedom that meant accountability to no one. That is what the word "autonomy" means in the Greek, *autos* for self, and *nomos* for law. If man, therefore, cannot be free from the confines of nature by means of *rationalism*, then he must do so by means of his imagination. And what great and savage lengths man has gone to attempt to secure this coveted freedom. This explains how we are left today with a culture that is no longer operating along the lines of Rene Descartes' "I think, therefore I am", but rather "I feel, therefore I am." If rationalism has done man no favors, then *irrationalism* must be the answer to secure man's freedom. And how evident this has become in Western culture today! Consider, for just a moment, how rational a conversation you can have with someone of the LGBTQ movement. Think of whether a rational, civil discourse is even possible, let alone a rational assessment of the arguments presented either for or against what they advocate. There is no rationalism, there is no philosophizing, there is no meaningful exchange, because it has all been thrown out the window in exchange for unbridled emotionalism and imagination—emotion and imagination which, coupled together, does not in any way comport with reality. We may as well call it *illogicism*. This is the world in which we find ourselves in, and knowing then the state of our world, the condition of Western thought, we are then able to understand why certain things take place; why the biblical conception of the family, of the human person, is attacked from all fronts; why Christians are persecuted for speaking nothing less than the truth revealed by God, etc. At the root of it all is the apostatized heart of man, which desires to be god, striving against God's revelation in creation and His Word. As Dooyeweerd wrote,

> It [all] issues from the religious root of our temporal life, namely, the heart, soul, or spirit of a person. Because of the fall into sin, the hearts of human beings turned away from God and the religious ground-motive of apostasy took hold of their faith and of their whole temporal life.[7]

---

7.   Dooyeweerd, *Roots of Western Culture*, 92.

THE WEST AND ITS DON QUIXOTIC SYNDROME

How to respond to such apostasy? How to respond to the rebellious heart which seeks to redefine the human person and his relational functions? The specifics I leave for our next speaker, since he wrote a book on the matter which I most highly recommend, *Autonomía Sexual en un Mundo Posmoderno*[8]—but let me continue to address the generalities, beginning first with an appropriate illustration of the West, from which we can then devise a response to.

## The Don Quixotic Syndrome

What illustration might I have in mind? Well, the title of my lecture surely must have given it away. I have in mind the illustration of Don Quixote and his squire Sancho Panza, which besides being a well-known literary figure and a classic for all those who speak the language of Miguel de Cervantes, is also a metaphoric picture depicting sinful man in the world of God. It may certainly not have been Cervantes' intention, but perhaps he wrote better than he knew. In fact, it was literary scholar Harold Bloom who stated that *Don Quixote* is more so a tragedy than a comedy, and is not the story of sinful man a tragedy?[9]

---

8. Translated to English, "Sexual Autonomy in a Postmodern World", the book authored by Joe Owen is forthcoming in English.

9. Harold Bloom, "Introduction" in *Don Quixote: A New Translation by Edith Grossman* (New York, NY.: HarperCollins Pub., 2003), xxiii.

Russian literary scholar Vladimir Nabokov provides an examination of *Don Quixote* in his posthumously published lecture series, and he writes that:

> Before he dubs himself Don Quixote, his name is plain Quijada, or Quesada. He is a country gentleman, owner of a vineyard, master's house, and two acres of arable land; a good Catholic (who will later evolve a bad conscience); a tall, lanky gentleman around fifty... [And] the man Sancho Panza. Who is he? A laborer who had been a shepherd in his youth, and then, at one time, a beadle to a brotherhood. He is a family man but a vagabond at heart....[10]

As you can see, Don Quixote and Sancho Panza are not painted as surreal figures, they were crafted as plain ordinary men, but as the story progresses they are afflicted with lunacy, it seems, for the reality they claim to live is altogether different than the reality they are faced with. I will return again to their madness, because there is something peculiar about the two of them that will serve well for our illustration, but to the first point I wish to make: Much like these fictitious men, sinful man *knows what reality is*, he knows the truth of all things based on the fact that he lives and breathes in God's world, but by suppressing the truth by his own sin nature (Rom. 1:18), he has erected in

---

10. Vladimir Nabokov, *Lectures on Don Quixote*, ed. Fredson Bowers (New York, NY.: Harcourt Brace Jovanovich, 1983), 13, 20.

Plate I of Gustave Doré's (1832-1883) illustrations to
Miguel de Cervantes' *Don Quixote*. From Chapter I.

its place an illusion that does not at all comport with
reality. Consider this chilling event for a moment: Today's statement by the radical autonomous man, in the
midst of a whole other slew of statements concerning
the nature of reality, is that "A biological male is not a
man, nor is a biological female a woman." In the US
confirmation hearing of Judge Ketanji Brown Jackson,
for example, which was recorded for public viewing,
the Senator Marsha Blackburn asked Jackson how she
would define the word "woman." A simple question
that ought to have had a simple answer. But the answer

Jackson gave was not at all an answer. To quote her, she said: "Can I provide a definition though? I can't. Not in this context, I'm not a biologist."[11] Que the laughs! Or wait? Is this more tragic than comedic?

According to the video provided by USA Today:

> Blackburn chided Jackson, claiming that "the fact that you can't give me a straight answer about something as fundamental as what a woman is underscores the dangers of the kind of progressive education that we are hearing about.[12]

I do not have time this morning to go into the specifics of the progressive education curriculums of our culture, all I will say is that it is both scandalous and depraved, seeping also into Catholic educational institutions which have succumbed to the state and now raise the rainbow flag in fear of losing their government funding. But to the matter I wish to address: Does the sinful man actually believe this illusion to be true? Does Jackson, in the cited example, believe what she says to be true? At the surface it seems so, it is, after all, what sinful man confesses, but in the depths of his heart,

---

11. Alia E. Dastagir, "Marsha Blackburn asked Ketanji Brown Jackson to define 'woman.' Science says there's no simple answer", *USA Today*. Accessed October 8, 2023, https://www.usatoday.com/story/life/health-wellness/2022/03/24/marsha-blackburn-asked-ketanji-jackson-define-woman-science/7152439001/.

12. Ibid.

man knows his illusion to be nothing more than a lie. His illusory world is just that, an illusion. And he is no different than Don Quixote in this respect, for Don Quixote believed in the illusory, he erected an illusion over reality and lived according to that illusion, but in his heart he never believed it. As Bloom writes,

> Does Don Quixote altogether believe in the reality of his own vision? Evidently he does not, particularly when he (and Sancho) is surrendered by Cervantes to the sadomasochistic practical jokes – indeed, the vicious and humiliating cruelties – that afflict the Knight and squire in part II.[13]

I will not trouble you with several examples from *Don Quixote*, but there is one in particular, summed up well by Nabokov, that serves as a clear illustration of the tension between illusion and reality. In chapter 18, we find that

> Don Quixote undergoes another attack of "strange madness" when he mistakes two flocks of sheep and the clouds of dust they raise for two mighty armies. Sancho protests:
>
> "Sir," he said, "may I go to the devil if I see a single man, giant, or knight of all those that your grace is talking about. Who knows? Maybe it is another spell, like last night."

---

13. Bloom, "Introduction" in *Don Quixote*, xxv.

Gustave Doré's (1832-1883) illustrations to Miguel de Cervantes'
*Don Quixote*. From Part 1, Chapter 8

"How can you say that?" replied Don Quixote. "Can you not hear the neighing of the horses, the sound of trumpets, the roll of drums?"

"I hear nothing", said Sancho, "except the bleating of sheep."[14]

You would think, at that moment, Don Quixote would come to realize that the armies he was charging

---

14. Nabokov, *Lectures on Dox Quixote*, 126-127.

were really sheep, and would admit his lunacy, his illusion, but no! Nabokov continues:

> "This," said Don Quixote, "is the work of that thieving magician, my enemy, who thus counterfeits things and causes them to disappear. You must know, Sancho, that it is very easy for them to make us assume any appearance that they choose; and so it is that malign one who persecutes me, envious of the glory he saw me about to achieve in this battle, changed the squadrons of the foe into flocks of sheep."[15]

When one asks whether the sinful man might be reasoned with, assuming that by man's rationality he could be brought to the truth and to forsake the lie, the answer is "No", not without the conviction brought about by the Spirit of God. For like Don Quixote, though there may be thoughts that make the sinful man waver from his course of philosophical lunacy, his "madness" (that is to say, "foolishness", to use the Scriptural term) is proven stronger than any other faculty.[16] As a matter of fact, all his faculties are subjected to his foolishness, and it requires a divine hand to free him from it. As Dooyeweerd writes,

> Only the Spirit of God causes the rebirth of our hearts in Christ and radically reverses the direction of our tem-

---

15. Ibid., 127.

16. Miguel de Cervantes, *Don Quixote: A New Translation by Edith Grossman* (New York, NY.: HarperCollins Pub., 2003), 24.

poral function of faith.[17]

Quixote is very much illustrative of the Free-dom-Nature ground motive that we find undergirding Western culture today. He fights and struggles against the true nature of things, seeking justice, seeking his own way of life, but totally missing the picture of what true justice and life is. As Bloom writes, "Don Quix-ote says that his quest is to destroy injustice. The final injustice is death, the ultimate bondage."[18] What in-justice does he have in mind but his own definition of injustice? And what can that greatest injustice be but to be subject to God's law and thus suffer under the curse of sin instead of living freely without any repercus-sions? Is that not what the Western man wants? Never mind Don Quixote, remember that he is a metaphoric picture for our purposes here. The Western man thinks that all he suffers as consequence of his sin is an injus-tice, and that the greatest injustice, the greatest bond-age, is death. He does not see that what he calls "in-justice" is actually "justice" in the eyes of God. What is man to expect when he has broken God's law and therefore committed cosmic treason against His Cre-ator? This irrationality, no, this *lunacy*, is the result of man asserting his radical autonomy, thinking that he is self-sufficient, thinking that he is not ultimately bound to God's law, and he perseveres in his rebellion, in his

17. Dooyeweerd, *The Roots of Western Culture*, 92.

18. Bloom, "Introduction" in *Don Quixote*, xxii.

disbelief, until death does him in. And when death finally does him in, if he has not repented, if he has not turned away from his sin, then he throws up his hands and says, "Fine, reality is as what God says it is, but I refuse to confess Him, and I refuse to yield to Him." His radical autonomy inevitably leads to his death, as it did for Don Quixote, for as Bloom writes, "When he ceases to assert his autonomy, there is nothing left... no action remaining except to die."[19]

If this is illustrative of Western man—in a general sense, of course—why is this of such concern to us? I had mentioned at the start of my lecture that what is taking place in our culture *should* concern us. And I had mentioned this because such godless ideas, the proposed *re-inventions* of God's created order, can certainly corrupt the church if the church is not wary against false teachings and philosophies. But there is another reason why we should be concerned, and it extends *beyond* the threat of our churches falling to the lie; it has, in fact, much to do with the projected destination of our culture. What was it that the prophet Jeremiah said to God's people while inspired by the Holy Spirit?

> Seek the welfare of the city where I have sent you into exile, and pray to the lord on its behalf, for in its welfare you will find your welfare (Jer. 29:7).

As we all know, the god of the West is no longer the God of Scripture, such a predominant Christian

---

19. Ibid., xxiii.

consensus has faded. Collectivized man, in the form of the state, now lays down the law as the independent sovereign, subject to, and accountable to *no one*. As the new god-substitute, as representative of its people, it has sought to redefine reality, to secure for man his much sought after "freedom", and this has been done through its attempted reinvention of marriage, the family, the human person, morality, etc. Those who do not comply with newly state-imposed norms are threatened with punitive measures, for how else can the state effectively implement obedience? Was it not Trudeau, our present Prime Minister, who said that Christians are not representative of modern-day Canada? Was it not Trudeau who said "Christians are the worst part of Canadian society?" He said that on March 28, 2017, in the House of Commons.[20] If you have not felt the breath of this sinful disposition of man on the back of your neck, you will soon. Such is the world we live in. It was the sixteenth-century reformer Dr. Constantino Ponce de la Fuente who wrote, in his *Exposition of the First Psalm of David*:

> Much has been said, yet it is the least of what there is. The treacherous world is not content with following its path and letting the poor soul follow his own; rather, it pursues him with great anger, and with tyrannical

20. "Letter to the Editor", *Medicine Hat News*. Accessed June 11, 2024, https://medicinehatnews.com/commentary/letters-to-the-editor/2018/07/23/where-does-jasonkenney-stand/.

hands, it draws him in, tramples on him, and mistreats him. It perpetrates countless injustices upon him, depriving him of life in a thousand ways, because it cannot tolerate anyone departing from its revelry, straying from its path, refusing to serve and obey its vanity, pursuing a virtue it does not follow, or approving and holding in high regard what its customs have already discredited and devalued.[21]

This is all most certainly intimidating, but while the West may portray an image of strength and sovereignty, it is in all actuality inching ever closer to its inevitable cultural implosion. How so? Well, you cannot possibly expect to remove the foundation upon which Western civilization is built and surmise that it will function all the same if not better. Remove the foundation of a house, or of a condominium, and sooner or later it will collapse. This is precisely what the West has done ever since the Enlightenment, and every time it has been much more bolder and daring in its attempt to remove its underlying foundation. Questions such as What is a person? What is a man? What is a woman? What is a family? What is good? What is evil? etc., no longer have definitive, objective answers. Any answer given is either offensive to someone somewhere, or totally lacking in substance that it ultimately means nothing, and the lat-

---

21. Constantino Ponce de la Fuente, *The Old Spanish Reformers, Vol. 27: Exposition of the First Psalm of David*, ed. Steven R. Martins (Jordan Station, ON.: Cántaro Publications, 2024), 55.

ter of the two is becoming more prominent with the increasing irrationalism of our culture. Consider the implications that follow: How can we possibly engage in conversation if we do not even know the meaning of the terms we are using? How can we understand reality and communicate truth?

We are witnessing in our present age the blurring of social and moral distinctions, the breakdown of societal function and of the moral framework that was once knit together by the biblical truth that gave early form to our civilizations. We are losing all meaning, and with the loss of meaning comes the loss of limitations. If all things are now permissible and tolerable, as it relates to sexual orientation and practice, to use such a representative example, how much longer until necrophilia and pedophilia are added to the list of accepted norms? At what point do we say, "Our culture is enroute to self-implosion?" And at what point will we realize that such a cultural implosion would affect us? If judgment falls upon our nation, we will certainly be caught up in it. There will be no doubt about that. For this reason, Jeremiah tells God's people to seek the welfare of the city where they have been sent (Jer. 29:7). They were sent to Babylon? Then pray for Babylon's wellbeing, because if judgment comes, it will also come upon the Jews who live there.

**Concluding Remarks**
Let me now bring my session to a close as we are now

running out of time. What are we then to do? How are we to respond to our present cultural moment? The answer to that question will be answered over the course of our time together today, but let me first begin with this: Let us be like the blessed man in Psalm 1:1-2, in which the Psalmist states:

> ¹ Blessed is the man
>   who walks not in the counsel of the wicked,
> nor stands in the way of sinners,
>   nor sits in the seat of scoffers;
> ² but his delight is in the law of the LORD,
>   and on his law he meditates day and night.

When Don Quixote began on his tragic journey of lunacy, he was very much representative of the modern Western man, gripped by his Nature-Freedom ground-motive. He became a madman and then roped in Sancho, who was an otherwise sane man, onto his adventures. It was Charles Spurgeon, the prince of preachers, who said that the first verse of Psalm 1 lays out for us the progression of the sinner.[22] He begins as one who walks in the counsel of the wicked, hiding his wickedness from plain sight, but walking in it nonetheless. He then stands in the way of sinners, which means he no longer hides his wickedness but now parades it all about (reminds of the Pride parade, what a fitting illustration!). And finally, he lands in the seat of scoff-

---

22 Charles Spurgeon, *The Treasury of David*, Vol. 1 (USA: Hendrickson Publishers, 1990).

Gustave Doré's (1832-1883) *Don Quijote de La Mancha and Sancho Panza*, 1863

ers, where he makes a mockery of everyone, and most especially of God. If Don Quixote was a scoffer, and he most certainly was with the way he mocked Sancho and the world around him, he traded places with Sancho, because as the tales nears its end, it is Don Quixote who comes to his senses and ditches the illusion with death being so near, while Sancho went from sane to a madman, and becoming even crueler than the man he was before.[23] Let us not be like the godless man, let us

23. Nabokov, *Lectures on Don Quixote*, 22.

not be like the man who walks in the counsels of the wicked, or who stands in the way of sinners, or who sits in the seat of scoffers. Let us not be like Sancho who was dragged from sanity to lunacy! Nor like Don Quixote! No, the Psalmist writes, "Blessed is the man who does none of these three things." And "Blessed is the man who delights in the law of the LORD, who meditates on it day and night."

Why do I suggest this as our starting point? Because how can we possibly expose the lunacy of our Western culture if we do not know God's Word? How can we speak prophetically to our society, calling its people to repentance and to the truth of God, if our delight is not in the Word? And how can we *not* delight in the Word? It is the Word that reveals to us God Himself. It is the Word which points us to the Christ, who is the Word made flesh (John 1:1-5). While sinful man wrestles with his vanity and futility, with the meaninglessness of his worldview, it is Christ who makes all things meaningful. It is Christ who gives unto man *true* freedom, that is to say, freedom to live as he was created to, in righteousness and holiness, set apart for the divine purposes of God. How can we not then delight in the Word? In the special revelation of God and the Word made flesh? It is the Word of God which furnishes us with the parameters by which we can rightly understand all of reality. As the reformer John Calvin had put it, it is the Word of God which serves as our "spectacles" through which we can see the world.[24] How else can we possibly speak with certainty? How else can we build towards a reformed church and a renewed culture? Without the Word of God, which serves as the only authoritative interpretation of God's creational revelation, it would be an impossibility. Such is the impediment of man's sin, and such is the power of the Word of God.

I close with these final remarks: *In an age of confusion, in a time of competing false worldviews, if we are firmly established and rooted in the Word of truth, not just the inspired Word but the Word made flesh, Jesus Christ, we will not only be able to demolish every argument raised up against the truth, we will also be able to advance the Christian philosophy of life.*

Let us be found faithful in our apologetic task.

---

24. John Calvin, *Institutes of the Christian Religion*, I.VI.I.

# Bibliography

Alcock, Deborah. 2020. *The Spanish Brothers*. Jordan Station, ON.: Cántaro Publications.

Arana, Marie. 2014. *Bolivar: American Liberator*. New York, NY.: Simon & Schuster.

Bahnsen, Greg L. 1998. *Van Til's Apologetic: Readings & Analysis*. Phillipsburg, NJ.: P&R Publishing.

_____. 2007. *Pushing the Antithesis: The Apologetic Methodology of Greg L. Bahnsen*. USA: American Vision.

Bavinck, Herman. 2015. "The Origin, Essence and Purpose of Man". In *Selected Shorter Works of Herman Bavinck*. Ed. John Hendryx. West Linn, OR.: Monergism Books.

Beeke, Joel R. 2019. *Reformed Systematic Theology, Vol. 1: Revelation and God*. Wheaton, IL.: Crossway.

Berkhof, Louis. 1932. *Introductory Volume to Systematic Theology*. Grand Rapids, MI.: Wm. B. Eerdmans Publishing Co.

Bloom, Harold. 2003. "Introduction". In *Don Quixote: A New Translation by Edith Grossman*. New York, NY.: HarperCollins Pub.

Boot, Joseph. 2016. *The Mission of God: A Manifesto of Hope for Society*. Toronto, ON.: Ezra Press.

_____. 2016. *Gospel Culture: Living in God's Kingdom*, Cornerstones Vol. 1. Toronto, ON.: Ezra Press.

Calvin, John. 1536. *Institutes of the Christian Religion*. Switzerland, Basel.

Dooyeweerd, Herman. 2012. *Roots of Western Culture: Pagan, Secular, and Christian Options.* Jordan Station, ON.: Paideia Press.

_____. 2021. *A New Critique of Theoretical Thought*, Vols. I-IV. Jordan Station, ON.: Paideia Press.

Frame, John M. 2015. *A History of Western Philosophy and Theology.* Phillipsburg, NJ.: P&R Publishing.

Friesen, J. Glenn. "Anastasis". Christian Nondualism. 2021. https://jgfriesen.wordpress.com/glossary/anastasis/.

Green, Steve and Jackie. 2017. *This Dangerous Book: How the Bible Has Shaped Our World and Why It Still Matters Today.* Grand Rapids, MI.: Zondervan.

Green, Toby. 2007. *Inquisition: The Reign of Fear.* New York, NY.: St. Martin's Press.

Hawking, Stephen. 1988. *A Brief History of Time.* New York, NY.: Bantam Books.

_____. "Gödel and the end of the universe". *Internet Archive: The Way Back Machine.* 2024. https://web.archive.org/web/20200529232552/http://www.hawking.org.uk/godel-and-the-end-of-physics.html/.

Hegeman, Cornelius. 2017. *La Reforma en America Latina y el Caribe.* Guadalupe, Costa Rica: Editorial CLIR.

Hutton, Lewis J. "The Spanish Heretic: Cipriano de Valera". *Church History.* Cambridge University Press. Vol. 27, No. 1 (March 1958).

Jaspers, Karl. 1932. *Die geistige Situation der Zeit (The Intellectual Situation of Our Time).* Berlin: W. de Gruyter.

Jones, Peter. 2004. *Gospel Truth, Pagan Lies: Can You Tell the Difference?* Escondido, CA.: Main Entry Editions.

_____. 2010. *One or Two: Seeing a World of Difference.* USA: Main Entry Editions.

Kinder, A. Gordon. 1975. *Casiodoro de Reina: Spanish Reformer of the Sixteenth Century.* London, UK., Tamesis Books Limited.

Koppenhaver, Carl E. and Martin Luther. 2024. *Martin Luther & the 95 Theses.* Jordan Station, ON.: Cántaro Publications.

Kuyper, Abraham. 1880. *Sphere Sovereignty.* Trans. George Kamps. The Netherlands: The Free University.

_____.1898. *Encyclopedia of Sacred Theology: Its Principles.* Trans. J. Hendrik De Vries. New York: Charles Scribner's Sons.

_____. 1998. *Abraham Kuyper: A Centennial Reader.* Ed. James D. Bratt. Grand Rapids: Eerdmans.

M'Crie, Thomas. 2023. *History of the Spanish Reformation: Progress & Suppression in the 16th Century.* Jordan Station, ON., Cántaro Publications.

Mangalwadi, Vishal. 2012. *The Book That Made Your World: How the Bible Created the Soul of Western Civilization.* Nashville, TN.: Thomas Nelson.

Martins, Steven R. 2020. *Apologetics: Studies in Biblical Apologetics for a Christian Worldview.* Jordan Station, ON.: Cántaro Publications.

_____. 2022. *Towards a Christian Understanding: The Pursuit of a Christian Philosophy.* Jordan Station, ON.: Cántaro Publications.

_____. "The Threefold Office of Man". In *La Fuente: Iberoamerican Journal for Christian Worldview.* Vol. 2, No. 1. Cántaro Publications (2022).

_____. 2023. *The Gospel (Foundations, Vol. I)*. Jordan Station, ON.: Cántaro Publications.

Mathison, Keith. "The Five Solas". *Reformation Bible College*. 2021. https://reformationbiblecollege.org/blog/the-five-solas.

Menéndez y Pelayo, Marcelino. 1880. *Historia de los Heterodoxos Españoles*. Madrid.

Mesa, Ivan E. "'Open Your Eyes, O Spaniards': Cipriano de Valera – A Forgotten Spanish Protestant of the 16th Century". *The Banner of Truth* (Feb. 2015).

Messmer, Andrés. 2023. *Casiodoro de Reina: Su vida, Biblia y teología: Ensayos en honor del 500 aniversario de su nacimiento*. Madrid: Editorial CLIE.

Nabokov, Vladimir. 1983. *Lectures on Don Quixote*. Ed. Fredson Bowers. New York, NY.: Harcourt Brace Jovanovich.

Nazir-Ali, Michael. 2008. *The Unique and Universal Christ: Jesus in a Plural World*. Colorado Springs, CO.: Paternoster.

Núñez, Miguel. 2016. *El Poder de la Palabra para Transformar una Nación*. Medellín, Colombia: Poiema Publicaciones.

Ouweneel, Willem J. 2014. *Wisdom for Thinkers: Introduction to Christian Philosophy*. Jordan Station, ON.: Paideia Press.

_____. 2017. *The World is Christ's: A Critique of Two Kingdoms Theology*. Jordan Station, ON.: Paideia Press.

Piper, John and David Mathis. "With Calvin in the Theater of God". *desiringGod*. 2024, https://www.desiringgod.org/books/with-calvin-in-the-theater-of-god/.

Ponce de la Fuente, Constantino. 2024. *The Old Spanish Reformers, Vol. 27: Exposition of the First Psalm of David*.

Ed. Steven R. Martins. Jordan Station, ON.: Cántaro Publications.

Price, Randall. 2007. *Searching for the Original Bible*. Eugene, OR.: Harvest House.

Rabbi Dr. I Epstein, ed. 1935. *The Babylonian Talmud, Seder Nezikin*, vol. IV, *Aboth*. London: The Soncino Press.

Reeves, Michael. 2010. *The Unquenchable Flame: Discovering the Heart of the Reformation*. Nashville, TN.: B&H Academic.

Runner, H. Evan. 2020. *Point Counter Point: Paideia Monographs*. Jordan Station, ON.: Paideia Press.

_____. 2021. *The Collected Works of H. Evan Runner, Vols. 1-4*: Jordan Station, ON.: Paideia Press.

_____. 2023. *The Relation of the Bible to Learning*. Jordan Station, ON.: Paideia Press.

Rushdoony, R. J. "Salvation and Godly Rule: Prophet, Priest & King." *Pocket College*. 2017. http://www.pocketcollege.com/transcripts/091%20-%20Salvation%20and%20Godly%20Rule/RR136AG62.html.

_____. 1973. *The Institutes of Biblical Law*. Phillipsburg, NJ.: P&R Publishing.

Sandlin, P. Andrew. 2001. *The Full Gospel: A Biblical Vocabulary of Salvation*. USA: Chalcedon Inc.

_____. 2013. *Christian Culture: An Introduction*. CA.: Center for Cultural Leadership.

Scoles, Sarah. "Will Scientists Ever Find A Theory Of Everything?". *Scientific American*. 2024. https://www.scientificamerican.com/article/will-scientists-ever-find-a-theory-of-everything/.

Seerveld, Calvin G. 1995. *A Christian Critique of Art & Literature*. Toronto, ON.: Toronto Tuppence Press.

Serrano, Rafael. "El Nuevo Testamento publicado por Juan Pérez de Pineda". *Medium*. 2024. https://medium.com/historia-de-la-biblia-en-espanol/el-nuevo-testamento-publicado-por-juan-perez-de-pineda-fe0bc608df5c

Sire, James W. 2004. *Naming the Elephant: Worldview as a Concept*. Downers Grove, IL.: InterVarsity Press.

Strauss, D. F. M. 2020. *Being Human in God's World*. Jordan Station, ON.: Paideia Press.

Spurgeon, Charles H. 1893. *The Gospel of the Kingdom: A Popular Exposition of the Gospel according to Matthew*. New York, NY.: The Baker & Taylor Co.

_____. 1990. *The Treasury of David, Vol. 1*. USA: Hendrickson Publishers.

The Neo-Calvinism Research Institute. "What is Neo-Calvinism?". *The Neo-Calvinism Research Institute*. 2021. https://www.neocalvinism.org/what-is-neo-calvinism/.

Troost, Andree. 2020. *What is Reformational Philosophy?: An Introduction to the Cosmonomic Philosophy of Herman Dooyeweerd*. Jordan Station, ON.: Paideia Press.

Tucker, Ruth A. "John Calvin and the Princess". *Christianity Today*. 2009. https://www.christianitytoday.com/history/2009/september/john-calvin-and-princess.html.

Tyndale, William. 1849. "Practice of Prelates". In *Expositions and Notes on Sundry Portions of the Holy Scriptures together with the Practice of Prelates*. Ed. H. Walker. Cambridge: Cambridge University Press.

Van Der Walt, Bernie. 2022. *Thomas Aquinas and the Neo-Thomist Tradition: A Christian-Philosophical Assessment*. Jordan Station, ON.: Paideia Press.

Van Til, Cornelius. 1963. *The Case for Calvinism*. Phillipsburg, NJ.: P&R Publishing.

———. 2003. *Christian Apologetics*, second ed. Phillipsburg, NJ.: P&R Publishing.

———. 2007. *An Introduction to Systematic Theology: Prolegomena and the Doctrines of Revelation, Scripture, and God*. Ed. William Edgar. Phillipsburg, NJ.: P&R Publishing.

———. 2024. *The Ten Commandments*. Jordan Station, ON.: Cántaro Publications & Paideia Press.

———. n.d. *Why I Believe in God*. (Philadelphia: Committee on Christian Education of the Orthodox Presbyterian Church.

Van Til, Cornelius and L. Berkhof. 1989. *Foundations of Christian Education*. Phillipsburg, NJ.: P&R Publishing.

Veith, Gene Edward. "The Protestant Work Ethic". *Ligonier Ministries*. 2024. https://www.ligonier.org/learn/articles/protestant-work-ethic.

Vermaseren, B. A. "Who Was Reginaldus Gonsalvius Montanus?". *Bibliothèque d'Humanisme et Renaissance*. Vol. 47, No. 1 (1985).

Wilson, Andrew L. "The Unfortunate Fate of Luther in the Ibero-American World". In *Studies in Luther*. USA: Lutheran Forum (Summer 2009).

# Index of Scriptures

## James

| | |
|---|---|
| 1:25 | 100 |

## 1 Peter

| | |
|---|---|
| 2:18-19 | 20 |
| 3:15 | 272 |

## 2 Peter

| | |
|---|---|
| 1:21 | 234 |

# ABOUT THE AUTHOR

**STEVEN R. MARTINS** is founding director of the Cántaro Institute and founding pastor of Sevilla Chapel in St. Catharines, ON. He has worked in the fields of missional apologetics and church leadership for over ten years and has spoken at numerous conferences, churches, and University student events. He has also contributed articles to *Coalición por el Evangelio* and the *Siglo XXI* journal of Editorial CLIR. Steven holds a Master's degree *summa cum laude* in Theological Studies with a focus on Christian apologetics from Veritas International University (Santa Ana, CA., USA) and a Bachelor of Human Resource Management from York University (Toronto, ON., Canada). Steven is married to Cindy and they live in Lincoln, Ontario, with their children Matthias, Timothy, Nehemías, and Raquel.

## ABOUT THE CÁNTARO INSTITUTE

*Inheriting, Informing, Inspiring*

Cántaro Institute is a reformed evangelical organization committed to the advancement of the Christian worldview for the reformation and renewal of the church and culture.

We believe that as the Christian church returns to the fount of Scripture as her ultimate authority for all knowing and living, and wisely applies God's truth to every aspect of life, her missiological activity will result in not only the renewal of the human person but also the reformation of culture, an inevitable result when the true scope and nature of the gospel is made known and applied.

www.ingramcontent.com/pod-product-compliance
Lightning Source LLC
Chambersburg PA
CBHW021610120626
46545CB00001B/156

* 9 7 8 1 9 9 0 7 7 1 7 4 3 *